RELATIONSHIP

RELATIONSHIP *Matters*

FOUNDATIONS FOR LASTING AND HEALTHY RELATIONSHIPS

DR. GUY GRIMES

CONTRIBUTION BY ROXANNA GRIMES

TATE PUBLISHING
AND ENTERPRISES, LLC

Published by Tate Publishing & Enterprises, LLC
127 E. Trade Center Terrace | Mustang, Oklahoma 73064 USA
1.888.361.9473 | www.tatepublishing.com

Tate Publishing is committed to excellence in the publishing industry. The company reflects the philosophy established by the founders, based on Psalm 68:11,
"The Lord gave the word and great was the company of those who published it."

Book design copyright © 2015 by Tate Publishing, LLC. All rights reserved.
Cover design by Gian Philipp Rufin
Interior design by Manolito Bastasa

Published in the United States of America

ISBN: 978-1-63418-050-4
1. Family & Relationships / Dating
2. Self-Help / General
15.01.08

To my family
and
to the students who have taught me about relationship matters

CONTENTS

INTRODUCTION

The content of this book is the culmination of years of marriage, marriage counseling, and life experiences. The expression "wow days and vow days" is a phrase that Roxanna and I have used to describe the essence of lasting relationships in the context of marriage. In order for relationships to last and flourish, there must be a basic understanding that the full gamut of human emotions will be displayed over time. The term *wow days* reflects the feeling that most people associate with marital bliss. The days where you wake up and say to yourself, "Wow! Isn't it great to be alive today and to spend my life with _____ [insert name of spouse here]." Relationships do not fail because of the abundance of *wow days*.

The second phrase *vow days* describes the times in all lasting relationships when we choose to remain committed because of the sacred vows of marriage. When experiencing vow days, it may feel like we made a horrible mistake in entering into this relationship. It might be a season when passion or emotions are waning or completely absent. In the immortal words of the Righteous Brothers:

> You never close your eyes anymore when I kiss your lips.
> And there's no tenderness like before in your fingertips.
> You're trying hard not to show it, (baby).
> But baby, baby I know it…
> You've lost that lovin' feeling

Vow days may be sustained periods of anger, conflict, isolation, withheld intimacy, neglect, subtle forms of abuse, or combination of all the above. Lasting relationships can and must survive, even the most difficult and painful periods. Tragically, many relationships never survive the days when the loving feelings are absent or when painful feelings are experienced. This is where vows really matter. You know, the ones such as "I promise to love and honor you, in good times and bad, in adversity and prosperity, in sickness and in health, so long as we both shall live." Every wedding I've attended or performed incorporates some variation of the above mentioned vows. But when it comes to living out commitments daily in the context of work, relationships, and life's difficulties, the aforementioned vows become obscured or forgotten.

By any honest assessment, it is evident that our culture in North America has failed miserably in its ability to sustain lasting relationships. According to the US Census Bureau, the divorce rate has bounced around between 40 and 50 percent in that past decade. Cohabitation is the relationship trend de jure; this idea is that it might help to advert a failed marriage but many studies report the opposite. Just two decades ago, golden wedding anniversaries, celebrating fifty years of marriage, were commonplace. Today, when a couple celebrates twenty-plus years of marriage, it is noteworthy. Many are delaying marriage until their late twenties or early thirties at times because they don't want to become a divorce statistic. At the rate we are currently progressing in another decade or so, we may be very hard-pressed to find many who will be celebrating marriages lasting forty years or more.

Another force that works against maintaining marital vows is a constant message bombardment from our culture that "you have a right to be happy." Let me say that I love the idea of happiness. I want happiness for my life. I want happiness for my wife and children and even for you! The problem with seeking personal happiness and self-fulfillment is often mutually exclusive. Relationships lived in close proximity frequently face circumstances where "in order for me to be happy and get what I want," it will preclude "happiness" or the "choice" of another.

In early stages of relationships, we are functioning in the realm of what I would call the "accommodating era." It's like going on a first date and trying to make a decision where to go to dinner. During the accommodating stage, often, the attitude of both parties is "I want whenever you want." Or deciding which movie to go see, the posture is usually, "I want to see whatever movie you want to see." However, relationships that are lived out over periods of months and years move beyond the accommodating stage. To complicate matters further, there are some individuals by nature take on nonassertive roles and relationships. Some individuals live in an unhealthy relationship to others called codependency, which we will discuss further in this book. The bottom line is that healthy relationships that will last must at some point move beyond self-fulfillment.

I did a study awhile back of the scriptures in relationship to the topic of happiness. I could only find one passage in the entire Bible referencing personal happiness as something related to God's will. In the book of Deuteronomy 24:5 (NIV), it states, "If a man has recently married, he must not be sent to war or have any other duty laid on him. For one year he is to be free to stay at home and bring happiness to the wife he has married." A simple interpretation of this text would indicate that is the role of a man to bring happiness to his wife for the first your marriage. A more detailed exegesis might reveal that for a period of time, husbands and wives are to serve one another for the purpose of temporal happiness.

While there may only be one passage in the Scriptures that speaks of happiness in relationship to God's will, there are many that indicate the role of holiness in relationship to the will of God. Author Gary Thomas in his work *The Sacred Marriage* asserts that a primary purpose of marriage for the believer is holiness. Thomas poses the question, "What if the ultimate purpose of marriage was holiness rather than happiness." Indeed, the statement in 1 Peter 1:15–16 "but just as he who called you is holy, so be holy in all you do; for it is written: 'Be holy, because I am holy'" reflects a life calling to holiness. If the concept that marriage is primarily about holiness is asserted to its logical conclusion, then we should all seek to marry the most difficult person we can find who's willing to marry us. Consider the Old Testament calling upon Hosea to take Homer to be his wife leaving behind her life as a prostitute. Now, there is a calling to holiness!

The concept of wow days and vow days is an approach to marriage where on difficult days in relationships we choose as an act of our will to focus on God's purposes in our lives to change us rather than our circumstances. It's like what Paul states in the New Testament to the church at Corinth. He asked three times for that the "thorn in the flesh" _____ to be taken away. He even went as far to call "the thorn" a messenger from Satan. It was his final conclusion that God's grace could be made perfect in the midst of his weakness caused by a circumstances rather than happiness because the circumstances had changed. Thus, the goal of our lives as followers of Christ is more about Him than us—His glory, His renown, His purposes.

Another example of the purpose of personal happiness versus choosing that which is right comes from the life of Jesus during the last hours of his life. In the garden at Gethsemane, Jesus was faced with the imminent torture, ridicule, and death—death on a cross! This prayer "not my will but your will be done" was demonstrated in a healthy loving relationship; there are times that we must surrender our personal happiness. There was nothing happy about his death and suffering. There was, however, a demonstration of his love and commitment to the Father.

It has been my experience over the past twenty-eight years of marriage that when I choose to keep my commitment to love my wife on the days that I don't feel like it (vow days), Wow days seem to come more frequently. I mentioned earlier I like the idea of being happy. Wow days are happy days.

In addition to the context of marriage, all lasting relationships are comprised of both of these extreme emotional experiences. Relationships between parent and child, brother and sister, employer and employee will all experience these variations. It seems that all earthly relationship can serve as "Holiness Tutors." God has designed all close relationships prior to marriage as practice. College students often bemoan that their roommate is an inconsiderate slob! After a few weeks of living in close proximity with another, even a close friendship can be taxed to the point of breaking. Most universities offer a "consolidation period" where new roomies can be found. The marriage relationship is a lifetime roommate, without the offering of a consolidation period. Tragically, many martial relationships in our day simply part ways and taking with them their personal possessions and leaving scars of brokenness.

The language and tone of this book is directed toward both single and married adults. Many of the illustration are from marriages; much of the application is directed to single adults. The biblical principles and application are relevant to all human relationships. The objective in penning this book is assist people in building and sustaining healthy lasting relationships. The following nine chapters will discuss areas that matter most when developing a foundation for aspects of relationship. Each concept is reveled in the Word of God. I have endeavored to present the concepts with real life illustration along with practical applications. Learning and implementing these principles consistency will empower earthly relationships to be lasting and healthy.

LEARNING TO LOVE

What the world believes love to be and the value of love within our lives, often runs contrary to long-lasting relationships. Let's examine this notion a little. Lyrics to popular songs often reveal what the world's thinking at a given moment about a given subject, or at least how the influential in society want us to think. I love quoting Tina Turner, so let's take a look at one of her songs now. "What's Love Got to do with It?" After it repeats its title in the lyric, it continues like this: "Got to do with it. What's love but a secondhand emotion?" She's not expressing a very high opinion of love, is she? Why do you think that might be? Could it be she's had hers bruised? And who needs a heart when it can be broken? How many times does that have to happen to you before you sour on the whole experience of love?

But what's the downside of believing that it's dandy to have relationships, but to wave away any involvement with heartfelt, heart inspired love, 'cause you might just get hurt. If you take Ms. Turner's approach to relationships, what do you have? I'm not completely sure what you do have, but I know what you don't. You don't have love. Now you could say you're just trying to live your life without risk. And that's a good thing, right?

However, in this case, to avoid risk means you avoid giving yourself emotionally to somebody, someone you enjoy spending time with, someone who probably enjoys spending time with you. Maybe you both enjoy flying kites, riding bikes, taking hikes, maybe helicopter flights. Or poetry that makes no sense.

Maybe he or she is truly putting you first. Keep someone like that at arm's length, I dare you. But if you manage, if your time with him or her is without real joy, real connection, then congrats, you've kept your heart protected as well as on the cool side of room temperature. But is this really how you want to live—with no risk, no vulnerability, no emotional reward? Isn't that itself grounds for a broken heart? But that thought aside, Ms. Turner's idea is that the way you avoid a broken heart is enter into loveless relationships.

It's time for an important definition. After I give it, we're going to break it apart and look at it a piece at a time. Again, Tina Turner says love is a secondhand emotion, but what's more impactful is that the world seems to agree with her. All those elements of a relationship that we generally think are meant for marriage and for a committed relationship are being taken casually. After knowing each other for just a few weeks, couples move in together, and even if they don't take that step, they're crawling into bed together. Love is not a casual thing. God tells us this in no uncertain terms in 1 John 3:16. "This is how we know what love is: Jesus Christ laid down his life for us. And we ought to lay down our lives for our brothers and sisters."

Love is the opposite of a casual, secondhand emotion. Love is a spiritual concept with many dimensions. Love proves itself through sacrifice. It endures through hardship and trials and it never gives up. First John 3:16 (NIV) states, "This is how we know what love is; that Jesus Christ laid down his life for us, and we ought to lay down our lives for others." Love isn't that we're willing to go shopping with someone, make them breakfast on the weekends, or wash their clothes (although that comes close). No. Love says we are willing to die for somebody. Throw ourselves in front of a bus, climb out on a ledge to retrieve them, face a raging fire to rescue them, to take the fall for their sake.

Although this could involve strong emotions, it doesn't have to. Sometimes, it's a conscious decision, one made with reflection and courage. I was listening to a Christian radio station last week when they told this true story. A thirty-year old mother was expecting her second child. She was five months along and all seemed to be going well when she was diagnosed with an aggressive form of brain cancer. Already in her neck and brain, it was inoperable. Her only hope to beat it was high doses of radiation and a lot of chemotherapy. There was a downside, however. All this treatment would kill her baby.

"I've lived a good life," she told the doctors. "It hasn't been as long as I would have liked, but I'm not going to sacrifice the life of my child just to live a little longer." Then she spoke directly to the doctors, "Don't do any treatment. Do you think I can live long enough to deliver my child?" He said yes. So she reiterated, "No treatment." She would just tough it out. God must have wanted that baby born, because it came a month prematurely, and her courageous mother lived only three days after the birth. She got to hold her baby.

In fact, that is one of the remarkable testimonies here. Mothers are never allowed to hold premature babies. It's too dangerous for the baby's little system to be out in the world exposed to bacteria and germs. The nurses had never seen anything like this—a woman choosing the life of a child over her own life. They let her do something they'd never done. They let her cradle the little guy in her arms. Her brother now cares for this baby.

"The most powerful image I have of my sister," he said, "is her holding her little premature baby, smiling down at him as only a mother can while in the midst of what had to be excruciating pain."

She said a bit later, "I've never been happier any other day in my life." That's love. Sure there were great emotions involved. There would have to be for happiness to overshadow such pain. And you may say people just love to perform courageous acts out of emotions surrounding children. But Christ going to the cross for His people was an act of the will. Love is an act of will; we choose to sacrifice on the behalf of someone else. That's not to say the will can't be accompanied by emotions, or even guided by them. It just should not be dominated by them.

Let's go back to scripture in Mark 14:35–36 when Jesus secluded Himself in the garden of Gethsemane. Remember his prayer there? Did he say, "Oh, God, I can't wait to get to Calvary? Bring it on." Not hardly. It actually went like this: "*Going a little farther, he fell to the ground and prayed that if possible the hour might pass from him. 'Abba, Father,' he said, 'everything is possible for you. Take this cup from me. Yet not what I will, but what you will.'*"

Not my will, but your will be done. And who did this "will of the Father" benefit? Jesus? Again, not hardly. It benefited us. You see, our love and our emotions can guide our actions, just as they guided Christ's, or they can be followed by actions as they were followed by Christ. That's why when we choose to behave in a ways that benefit others, that's loving them in the truest sense of the word. Now, if your emotions are pointed in the same way as your loving sacrifice, that's a real bonus. For instance, when Corrie Ten Boom and her family were hiding Jews from the Nazis during World War II, her emotions, her desire to keep these people safe from certain murder was absolutely in line with her actions. But Jesus also demonstrates you can make a choice that benefits other people out of love without feelings determining our choices.

You think Jesus wanted to go to the cross? That as the nails were being driven into his hands, under His breath, he chanted, "Bring it on, bring it on. I can't wait to get hung up there. It's going to be so cool!" His crucifixion certainly wasn't recorded that way. "Take this cup from me. Yet not what I will, but what you will." It just shows that Jesus was in His right mind; only someone who wasn't would want this form of death.

Or do you think that thirty-year old mom with brain cancer emotionally wanted to just hold her baby for three days? Wouldn't you think she'd want to see the little guy take his first steps, go on his first date, graduate from high school, then college, then see him holding in his arms a baby of his own? Do you think she actually wanted to trade her life for her baby's? Maybe there were even days when her desire to live took over and she actually questioned her decision. "What? Am I nuts? I'm going to die. I don't know about all this. The cancer just hurts too much. Maybe I should have the chemo, maybe the radiation would help."

Questioning sacrifice is probably true of all us earthly creatures. When true love is involved, Voddie Baucham says, the choices we make always lead to actions on the behalf of, actions that benefit, those we love. Emotional love is guided by that notion; meaning, the emotions and actions are both there. It's Valentine's Day and you love her more than you can possibly express so you buy two dozen roses and write a mushy note—emotions and actions are in concert. That's why it's problematic for people who perceive themselves being in a long-term relationship—marriage, long-term dating, or co-habitation—and they wake up one morning and realize the love's gone. What happens to the relationship?

It dies. People in troubled relationships say that all the time. "I just don't love him anymore" or "There was a time I just couldn't get enough of her. Now being with her is like being with a mannequin. I don't feel anything." And that's what they feel—nothing. If there's no commitment to the relationship beyond the mere feelings, or if the relationship's not grounded in the spiritual concept of love, when the feelings go, which they will, the relationship goes with them.

So, if you think you love someone, but the emotion dies, did you love that person in the first place? Will you ever love that person again? Love is an emotion that can vacillate. It's there, then it's not, then it's there again, then it's not, then, lo and behold, here it comes again. When it's not there, it can be replaced by boredom, irritation, rage. The point to emotional love is if you're carrying it into marriage, or some other long-term commitment, make sure you both understand you are in it for the long haul and that the emotion called "love" will come and go.

Let's put this in the context of our relationship with God. If you're a Christian, which I hope you are, and someone asks you if you love Jesus, you wouldn't hesitate but say, "Yes!" We can stand in church on Sunday and sing:

> Everyday with Jesus is sweeter than the day before.
> Everyday with Jesus we love him more and more.
> Jesus saves and keeps me, and he's the one I'm waiting for,
> Everyday with Jesus is sweeter than the day before.

I can speak to friends and tell them how much I love the Lord. But on an emotional or feeling level, every day when I wake, I do not feel that same intensity of love. There are seasons and times in our lives when we don't feel love intensely. Some days are just harder than others. And on the harder days, maybe our relationship with God and Jesus hits rough spots too. That doesn't mean the relationship was never there or love was never present. That's why we also have songs where we cry out like King David and beseech the Lord to reveal Himself to us, to come and give the comfort we so desperately need. Because the sweet, sweet feelings of connection have gone; we know not where, and we fervently want them back. But what if this sense of separation persists over a long period, or if we're angry with the Lord and refuse to communicate with him for years at a stretch? Does that mean we're not living in a right relationship with God?

Our relationship with God is not secure because of our love for God; it's dependent upon His love for us. You see, it's not our emotions that put us in a right relationship with Him. You can accept God's grace, mercy, and forgiveness *apart* from strong emotions although there are emotions involved. Our eternal security is not dependent upon us. It's dependent upon him.

That's true of any relationship, really. Let me explain from experience. Most of you aren't parents yet. So the truth of what we'll describe may not become real to you until you have children of your own. It didn't to me. With children or other relationships, your relationship with them remains strong even though it may only go one way. For instance, your kids can behave in hurtful ways or become angry with you and say things that really sting—maybe even raise so much ire in you, you want to abandon them. But the relationship remains intact. It may not be your favorite thing; you may cringe the moment you think about it, but it doesn't change the fact that you love them, and you'd fall under a truck for them.

I knew the Bible taught that. I knew that Ephesians 2:8 (NIV) tells us, "For it is by grace you have been saved, through faith—and this is not from yourselves, it is the gift of God–not by works, so that no one can boast." I knew that Romans 5:8 (NIV) made God's demonstration of His love very clear: "But God demonstrates his own love for us in this: While we were still sinners, Christ died for us."

I also knew from Romans 8:35 (NIV). "Who shall separate us from the love of Christ? Shall trouble or hardship or persecution or famine or nakedness or danger or sword? As it is written: 'For your sake we face death all day long; we are considered as sheep to be slaughtered.'" No, in all these things we are more than conquerors through him who loved us. For I am convinced that neither death nor life, neither angels nor demons, neither the present nor the future, nor any powers, neither height nor depth, nor anything else in all creation will be able to separate us from the love of God that is in Christ Jesus our Lord. Could God's robust love be stated more strongly?

But I never really understood the emotional element to this eternal equation until I was the father. It's the unconditional love of marriage and children, of God for us. In marriage, there are days when love permeates you, floods you. Those are the walking on air days, the wow days. Then there are other days we just stayed married because it benefits the other person, and we've made a commitment to the relationship. My actions then are accompanied by emotion but not guided by them; I'm not going to merely choose to love my wife on the days I feel like it. And

I'm not going to choose to demonstrate my love for God only on the days I feel like it. Because some days, I feel He's just not there, which really means, I'm not there.

There are also some days you don't feel love the same way as you did the day, week, or month before—remember, love's an emotion and vacillates. But vacillation doesn't change the relationship. It may seem like it's changed, but all that perception is on our side. When it comes to our relationship with God, our security in it has nothing to do with our actions but God's actions on our behalf—Jesus's sacrifice on the cross, His gift of faith to us and who He is—that there is no shadow of turning with Him. The hammer ringing as it hits the nails driven into Jesus's flesh two thousand years ago, still rings today, and where it rang for you then, it rings for you now.

There's no other relationship on earth like that, the one between us and God. People aren't that steady, that committed, that giving. You can wrong or ignore me regularly, or even once, and I'm going to experience bad feelings about you and I may even treat you differently. But God, thankfully, is full of mercy and grace; he gives us not what we deserve. Are you full of mercy? I'm not. We may be merciful sometimes, and when we are, it is Christ working through us. None of us are as God is—full of mercy.

I believe to love this way, to love by taking actions that benefit the object of your love, is for us, a learned behavior. We have to work at it. And because it's a learned behavior and not one that comes naturally, when the word "love" creeps into a relationship, it's important both of you know how you are defining it. Is it as the Lord defines it 1 John 3:16—Christ having laid down his life for the object of His love; we who God gave Him—or is one of us defining it differently?

In premarital counseling, I often ask, "Why are you getting married? Why do you want to spend your life with her? Why do you want to spend your life with him? And the one answer I don't accept is: "I love them." That answer's meaningless. We've just seen how love vacillates—on one day, off the next. I want to hear that you admire something about your intended; there's something about him or her that's honorable, Christ-like. Love? I loved somebody else before I married my lovely wife. She loved a couple guys before she married me. She was even engaged to one of them. Love comes and goes and comes back and leaves, then returns. You can't base a future on such shifting sand.

What makes all this shifting sand develop some rigidity, some steadiness, some rock-like qualities? Commitment. You have the ability. I have the ability. All God's children have the ability and the capacity to love more than one person. And often we do. But what then brings the commitment, the actual act of love?

Those are the answers that appear when I tell them, "I love you," doesn't work, and they have to identify the reasons they want to spend their lives with that person they sit next to. That's the nitty-gritty. And it all stems from the fact that we see marriage as permanent, a relationship that weathers storms, remains steady in earthquakes, and dry when the levies break. Does that mean these committed relationships are both strong like iron and just as cold and unfeeling? Definitely not. Usually the deep, resilient commitment produces a love that's just as deep and just as resilient. You become bound by a love tested in the forge of the day to day warfare in which godly people are engaged.

There are other answers to that question that should raise the caution flag too. "They need me" is one. Another is, "They made me whole." Or "They lift me up so I can soar with wings like eagles." There are probably others that come to mind as you read this. Whatever they might be, they're based on emotions. Again, I'm all for the emotion of love. I just believe it should accompany our actions, rather than direct them. Because emotions waver, are unsteady, and they lead to the metaphor of the broken heart, our *achy-breaky heart*. And shouldn't it? Don't we say, "I love you with all my heart." Isn't it the metaphor for love in our culture? It was also a metaphor for love in the Greek culture. That's why *cardia*, the Greek word for heart, shows up so much in the scripture. If we allow emotion and metaphors to direct our actions, then in a very real sense, it's like emotional and metaphorical love is the engine propelling a river boat. When it fails, the boat's adrift, and in danger running aground. But if love is a willing passenger on the river boat propelled by commitment, the engine never fails, and the boat keeps chugging along.

When Roxanna and I stood at the altar and exchanged marriage vows before God. I had not used the expression "I love you," and she had not expressed those words to me. Do we recommend this approach? Not highly. But there was a reason for it. God was at work in both of us and teaching both of us—each differently. Roxanna had a deeply emotional and pretty significant story about how giving way to emotion had nearly taken her life. They left her dealing with emptiness, brokenness, and all the accompanying scars. Roxanna was determined she would never again commit her life to another man solely based on feelings and empty words. Roxanna expresses her journey this way:

> God took me for a season and made Himself known to me—first in a way that said I could attach myself to Him, and then trust Him to bring the man He wanted for me, without me having to chase the guy down. And God brought this Guy—no pun intended—into my life. And, yes, I had feelings, strong feelings, emotions that didn't even appear in the same dictionary as what I had experienced before. But it wasn't the emotion that drove me to the altar.
>
> It was my trust in God. This is the man He gave me. And no matter what comes down the pike, I know that I can trust God, which meant I can trust this Guy He's given me. And together we will grow in our understanding of what it means for God to be on the throne of our lives. No matter what comes, Christ is our resource, and with His power in our lives we will certainly make it through. Which we have and continue to do."

For me the journey was different. I had told every girl I dated that I loved them. So when we took our wedding vows I wanted to rise above what I had, over the years, made a meaningless phrase. But that was only part of making a commitment to one another. You've heard the song, "To All the Girls I've Loved Before" by Willie Nelson and Julio Iglesias. Here's the first verse:

> To all the girls I've loved before
> Who travelled in and out my door
> I'm glad they came along
> I dedicate this song
> To all the girls I've loved before

The only commitment to all these ladies was to make sure the door hinges were always oiled and never failed. That said, our journey to the altar took twenty-eight years. I had abused it just about every step of it. When the time comes to truly commit, I wanted to use the words of commitment and not a word I'd thrown around without it. Roxanna didn't want to hear that word without commitment either. God was orchestrating everything. Again, this approach won't work for everyone. But we talked about why we didn't use that word in the context of us. We were open, direct, and truthful.

My wife Roxanna articulated this concept to a group of college students by saying, "I needed a man who was going to commit to me and not use love to manipulate and hurt. My soul had been ravaged by that and I certainly didn't want that again. The bottom line principle is we knew God had brought us together and He brought us together for both our good in Him."

We are three part beings; we all have a soul that is made up of the mind, the will, and the emotion. Notice emotion is last, because God didn't give them to us for it to be the driving force in our lives. Emotion is voluntary, which means we never know when feelings, like love, are going to visit or when they're going to take the last train for the coast.

Our emotions accompany what happens in the mind and the will. If we go to the mind, we have Romans 12:2 (NIV). "Do not conform to the pattern of this world, but be transformed by the renewing of your mind. Then you will be able to test and approve what God's will is—his good, pleasing and perfect will."

Then we have the spirit, the Holy Spirit, which comes from God and is God. Which means, the scripture say, God inhabits our mind—be ye transformed by the renewing of your mind. True change in my mind only occurs when the spirit makes it happen as I allow it to. So then in the will, which is Philippians 2:13 (NIV): "For it is God which works in you both to will and to do of his good pleasure." God works in you to give you the desire and the power to do what pleases him. To grind the point even sharper, the Spirit of God, who inhabits you because you are a Christian, gives your will the ability to choose what pleases him. These two, mind and will, are what bring balance to emotion. The power of the Holy Spirit can transform us by renewing our mind, and he's working in our will to make us have the desire and the power to do what pleases him—emotion is balanced. Therefore, love is an act of my will, which is based on the truth of who God is and who God is in me and the object of my love. Based on those truths, emotion will accompany the mind and will but will not drive them. Let's look at it one more way.

"Peace I leave with you, my peace I give unto you: not as the world giveth, give I unto you. Let not your heart be troubled, neither let it be afraid" (John 14:27, KJV). This verse points like Valentine's arrow at the emotions. God's leaving you a gift. And what's the essence of this amazing gift? Peace of mind and heart. And it's a peace He gives that the world will not and cannot give you. So don't be troubled; don't be afraid. No matter what comes down the marriage pike, even if there's been a breach—even if one of you has breached the covenant—God can still give you peace. Peace, therefore, can actually become a stabilizing factor in one of the greatest times of turmoil. We've already seen how he's working in the mind and the will, and now the emotions are there to give us peace of mind and a quiet, peaceful heart. But the mind and will must be engaged. Peace of mind and heart follow the will. They don't drive it. And it's right there in the language of our wedding vows. "I, Tom Jones, take you Sally Smith, to be my wife, to have and to hold from this day forward, for better, for worse, for richer, for poorer, in sickness and in health, to love and to cherish; from this day forward until death do us part." Just about every vow spans both good times and bad—wealth and poverty, sickness and health, adversity and calm—whatever the Good Lord brings, loyalty and steadfastness will be the guiding principle. Now, read the vows again and pay particular attention to the concept we've just presented—God at work in the mind and will, giving the gift of peace of mind and heart as He does. It makes you wonder who put these vows together in the first place, because the concept has been there right in front of us from the beginning, whether we understood what they meant or not.

When I commit to do a couple's wedding, I ask them if they understand what they're saying when they recite these vows—do they know what they're getting? "You are going to be committed to each other whether life gets better or not." Of course, what's good now might just get better later on. But the "for better or worse" question is just one of them.

One question to ask is have you looked at the person honestly in the context of your vows, and how God defines love in 1 John 3:16—laying down your life for your spouse? They must realize that if they think it's only going to get better and they'll love their spouse more and more each passing butterfly and rainbow invested day, don't marry them. At this stage of most relationships, it's all about accommodation. It's okay if he's a little irritable at night when he gets home; it's okay she leaves the bathroom a mess before I get up. If he or she is not absolutely perfect right now, if you're accommodating here and accommodating there, this is as good as it's going to get—right now. You must understand that. If you're going into marriage thinking all those accommodations are only temporary because you're going to change that spouse, you're relying on an unsecured expectation. Certainly, God changes people. He can change people's hearts; He can change them radically from the inside out. People can even change themselves. But not usually. And if they do change, it may not be the way you want. That's why I often hear years or even months later, "That person's just not the person I married." They wouldn't be saying it unless that person's changed for the worse. People do sometimes in the marriage context. They make bad choice, old angers and resentments take over, fears for their emotional safety erupt. If these negative changes do occur, does love not apply now? Are the vows suddenly voided? They do cover good times and bad, sickness and health, adversity and calm, poverty and prosperity. It looks to us like the vows—our commitment— stands.

Let's take a look at Dr. Sternberg, Yale University. Regrettably, Dr. Sternberg of Yale University is not a Christian and makes no claim as to the spiritual efficacy of his findings, but he's got it figured out. He describes "love" as a triangle—three sides. Let's take a look at each side and how it relates to the other two.

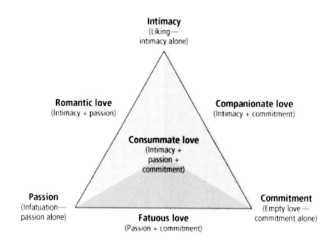

Passion
Dr. Sternberg "Love Diagram"
Commitment

Let's look at Passion first. It's the easiest to understand. It's our "love" feelings and could be emotional and/or physical passion as in the word "erotica." Allow me to confess to a young man's folly. I call it Passion 101. Her name was Yuki, and she worked at a perfume counter. Perhaps I was influenced by the subtle fragrances surrounding dear Yuki, but I found her stunning. Clearly enraptured, I stepped up to the counter and said, "Do you want go on a date after work?"

"What do you want to do?" she asked, eyes wide and accepting.

I drank in those eyes and said in all sincerity, "Let's get married." And in my dizzy, endorphin soaked, smitten, emotionally hijacked state, I meant it. Thank God she possessed a brain and only laughed.

We've all been there, maybe on a ski slope or at Starbucks, maybe even that same perfume counter when we've been erotically or sensually aroused by someone who just exudes something we respond to. And when that happens, our passions pile up right there before us into all kinds of levels. We're smitten. It's temporary but definitely passion—the fire flares, then just as quickly, dies to cold embers.

Another side is intimacy. Getting it absolutely right, Sternberg says there's more to love than just feelings and physical attraction; there's intimacy. Intimacy is your ability to trust and be secure with the object of your love. It means, you can let them see you on the inside. To illustrate this meaning, he coins the pronunciation "in-to-me-see." It's about making yourself vulnerable. It takes emotional courage to open up to the other person, to share elements of your life you want to hide from others. It's just none of their business. But you feel comfortable making it the business of this other person. You want that person to know you and how you honestly feel about important issues in your life. That sense of safety in vulnerability is being intimate with someone. That's nothing new in that. It's why those people we're willing to share deep, personal elements of our lives with is generally a pretty short list. Perhaps there's only one name on it. People not on that list we never touch, never hold hands, never hug. We touch physically only those people with whom we feel emotionally and physically safe. I'm not saying that's true for all people, but generally speaking, people who are emotionally, and certainly physically, unsafe, can stay away from me. I don't want them close, I don't want them to touch me, and I'm certainly not going to share with them what going on with me deep down.

Now, for the foundation as we've been saying all along, Dr. Sternberg reiterates the foundation that holds all this together in a love relationship is commitment. And he also agrees with us when he labels "commitment" an act of the will. And that's not a stretch at all. When you commit to something—a person, a group, an action, anything—you do it with your will. You make a conscious choice. For instance, when you commit to marry someone or lease a piece of property or follow through on a promise, it's a commitment that comes from the will.

When a young man or woman joins the military may be one of the best examples of willful commitment. When you join the military, you take a vow, you stand at respectful attention with others joining that moment, you raise your right hand as if in court and take a vow—a pledge. To what? To uphold and defend the constitution of the United States of America and to uphold and defend the honor of whatever part of the military they're joining. They commit their lives and sacred honor. And afterward, when their voices have died away, no one comes back to anyone there and asks them how they feel about what they'd just done. It is a done deal. Feelings are left elsewhere.

I was at a military base just a short time ago for an amazing service. The young men in attendance had just finished eight weeks of intense training. And on their last day, they went on an eight-mile hike, carrying an eighty-five-pound pack. After eight weeks, seven days a week, twelve hours a day of being beaten, battered, and bruised of crawling, running, being gassed, and fired at, my sense of it was they were just wiped out and physically broken down.

They'd just returned from this eight-mile hike, and they were tired, hungry, and most of them were sick. I saw five hundred guys hacking and coughing, taking in as much oxygen as their bodies allowed. After that hike, they were told to sit in this service for the next two hours. No one questioned the order. No one threw his gear to the ground and said they'd had enough. They just obeyed. And you might think that after an eight-mile hike, they'd want to sit there and snooze but woe to anyone who fell asleep, or even looked like they might.

They'd been trained to do what they were commanded to do. They'd taken a vow to do as they were commanded to do, and they satisfied their vow with commitment and honor. From the very beginning to the very end, their answer was, "Sir, yes, sir!" No one asked them how they felt about it and they didn't retort, "I got up this morning about four and went for an eight-mile hike. I am very tired so I'm done for the day!" Nobody cared how they felt; they made a commitment, and they are held to it.

Much in life operates this way. One aspect of lasting human love reflects this concept. Of course, if your courtship feels more like boot camp than romance, you might want to rethink some things. But back to commitment, the world has also figured it out that it is vital. Sternberg says it keeps relationships going. Passion and intimacy—your feelings—are definitely part of it, but they neither drive it nor hold it up. The foundation is *commitment*.

I'd like to introduce another definition of love that Paul gives us in 1 Corinthians over the centuries; it's come to be known as the *love chapter*.

> If I speak in the tongues of men or of angels, but do not have love, I am only a resounding gong or a clanging cymbal. If I have the gift of prophecy and can fathom all mysteries and all knowledge, and if I have a faith that can move mountains, but do not have love, I am nothing. If I give all I possess to the poor and give over my body to hardship that I may boast, but do not have love, I gain

nothing. Love is patient, love is kind. It does not envy, it does not boast, it is not proud. It does not dishonor others, it is not self-seeking, it is not easily angered, it keeps no record of wrongs. Love does not delight in evil but rejoices with the truth. It always protects, always trusts, always hopes, always perseveres. Love never fails. But where there are prophecies, they will cease; where there are tongues, they will be stilled; where there is knowledge, it will pass away. For we know in part and we prophesy in part, but when completeness comes, what is in part disappears. When I was a child, I talked like a child, I thought like a child, I reasoned like a child. When I became a man, I put the ways of childhood behind me. For now we see only a reflection as in a mirror; then we shall see face to face. Now I know in part; then I shall know fully, even as I am fully known. And now these three remain: faith, hope and love. But the greatest of these is love.

1 Corinthians 13:1–13 (NIV)

Read through it again. Stop at each one of the admonitions and think about what the action truly means. For instance, "Love does not delight in evil but rejoices with truth." So if you and yours love thrill in shoplifting, that's not love, no matter what you tell your parole officer. One thing you'll notice, particularly in the middle verses, is they're all actions—things we do. One of my favorites says, "Love keeps no record of wrongdoing." Another translation says, "Love doesn't notice when others do it wrong." That's an action, or an action to take no action. They're all actions even though patience or longsuffering is something I feel quite strongly and being kind is also primarily feelings. Even so, longsuffering is an act of the will as is kindness, especially when it would be extraordinary to be kind in a given situation. In 1 Corinthians 13, God defines love as an action, or a host of related actions—things we do.

In addition to the actions, feelings, and all else we've talked about, sometimes, instead of loving as God would have us love, we substitute something the world has created. We insert the adjective *unconditional* before the word love, and we think we've achieved godly love. In this case, the word *unconditional* means mind, benevolence; actions toward you are not contingent upon whether you give love to me.

We get this notion of unconditional love from Romans 5:8 where it says God demonstrates his love for us in that while we were still sinners, Christ died for us. He didn't wait for us to be His buddy or friend, or like Him in any way at all before he died to save us. That's the way God loves us. And if we love others the way God loves us, how can our love be wrong? Unconditional must be an element in God's love for us, so unconditional love for others must be right. Of course, without the power of God, without our walk with God's Spirit, there is no unconditional love. There's no love at all.

Of course, we'd like to change these "faux lover's" minds. And what's the first step in doing that? We need to first love them God's way. They need to see what godly love is through our example. When we do this, folks experience Christ through us, His grace and respect for them; they then maintain their dignity as they make their own choices.

Of course, we need not take the high road. We could, after all, manipulate them. It's not that hard to do. We take actions that ease them into taking other actions, which we like. In fact, let's not stop at "like." We can get them to take actions we love. Then we justify loving them back. But two wrongs confronting their faux love with manipulation never have made a right. We need to meet them with the truth of godly love.

In the next chapter, we're going to cover this; behaviors we slip into relationships that reflect love back to ourselves. To say it another way, I manipulate you to behave in such a way that I feel you love me. This has nothing to do with loving you. It's all about loving me.

But the love we've described in this chapter is *not* self-centered; it's other centered love, just like God's love for us. If we're going love like God loves, we focus our affections, emotions, and mind not on what returns to us but on what we are giving. One of my favorite authors is Elisabeth Elliott. Her pivotal story was depicted in the movie *The End of the Spear.* As wife of Christian Martyr Jim Elliott, she has written several books. Her first, which details Jim Elliott's death while he and four other brave missionaries tried to reach the Huaorani tribe of eastern Ecuador, is *Through Gates of Splendor.* Both movie and book show us strikingly what God's love truly means. She has coined the phrase *God's love is summarized by the expression of my life for yours.* "My life for yours." Not your life for mine, or your affection for mine. And, as we have in this chapter, she formulates this concept from 1 John 3:16: "This is how we know what love is: Jesus Christ laid down his life for us." If we're going to love others the way God loves us, we have to personify. I'm not here to gain from you. I'm not here to change you so you do what I love. I'm here for you. Just as God first loved us by giving His life for us, he meets us where we are, accepts us as we are.

Then he changes us. One more time. He accepts us as we are and then He changes us from the inside out as only God can. We often accept people as they are and then try to change them later. Well, not that much later. But our changes are merely a manipulation of their behavior. Healthy relationships are not based on one trying to change the other into who the first wants them to be. Even if the changes might be for the good.

I meet many in counseling who say, "If only he would blah, blah, blah, all would be well. We wouldn't have a problem in the world. We could skip into the future fulfilled." And they're probably right. If their spouse would just make those changes—stop drinking, stop gambling, stop eying other women, be more committed to his job—their marriage would sparkle. But being right doesn't matter. What matters is to understand that only God can change people in a lasting way from the inside out. And changes we try to make, usually through manipulation, only steers our lives down unhealthy paths.

And when we do manipulate change, we assume the change has brought fulfillment. But it hasn't. Actually, we've taken on a role only God can fill. We're pretending we're like God. In healthy relationships, this behavior can usher in codependence. We take on the challenge of changing people by manipulation, sometimes in subtle ways, and in doing so, we boot God from the throne of our relationship. We stand where only God can legitimately stand. And when we occupy that place, we may limit what He can do for you.

But when we step out in faith and love people in a way that benefits them and not us, then God may have the freedom to do the work that only He can do in people's lives.

HEALTHY DEPENDENCY

This chapter will examine relationships and dependency. Let's go back to the garden. God created Adam with all that Adam needed—food, a job, and best of all, an exclusive relationship with God. But God knew he needed more. Genesis 2:18 tells us "And the LORD God said, '*It is* not good that man should be alone; I will make him a helper comparable to him.' He said, it's not good that you should be alone, and then he said he would create for Adam a suitable helpmate—Eve"(NIV). I want to start here as we deal with the issue of *wholeness* or *completeness*. God has designed us for relationships to meet certain life needs.

Adam really had it going on in the garden, but by God's own assessment, Adam needed someone of his own kind to help him and so that he would not be alone. Unfortunately, soon thereafter, the issue of *relationships* became distorted. Needing somebody by God's design to help and be a part of God's plans became "we need somebody in our life in order to be okay." Although only a few words separate those two statements, the gap between their meanings is huge.

I attended a Christian Conference Center years ago and a speaker took the position that we were only half beings until we found that person to make us whole, which means, if you're an individual, single person, you're not okay. You've been created with "things" missing. And you can't be all the person God wants you to be and still be single; you'll be walking around a spiritual cripple until someone brings those "things" to your life. In fact, the theory has a name: the two halves theory. It says you're half a person and only until you find your right match are you whole, or complete. Now let's think this through. What issues are associated with that theory?

What if we get hit flattened by a bus before we meet Mr. or Ms. Added parts. We die incomplete. Or, since there's only one person out there with the right additional parts, what if we, in our ignorance, choose the wrong mate? Now that person is bolting onto us all the wrong parts, and the person whose mate he or she should have been, will go partless for the rest of his or her life.

We can see very quickly the absurdity of this notion. But more than that, I challenge you to find anything in scripture that supports that notion, that if you fail to meet and marry Mr. or Ms. Other-half-made-for-you-in-heaven, you're doomed to unhappiness and an ever-present sense of not being all there. If you find it in the Bible, let me know, because I've failed to so far.

In fact, scripture seems to tell us that people have the capacity to love more than once. Perhaps even you, as it has been with many, have had more than one love relationship in your lives, and if you're married, perhaps you've even been engaged before.

My lovely wife was engaged twice before she met me. We were twenty-eight when we got married, which means we'd experienced a little singleness before our big day. If you're reading this book, then you're probably in your twenties and not married. You may have already met someone; you may have even had deep feelings of love and thought this was the person you'd spend your life with. But for whatever reason, it didn't work out. We'll talk about these types of situations. The underlying point is, if you believe there's only one person who can actually complete you, then when you do "fall in love," there's a lot of pressure to make sure the relationship works, even when there's good reason that it shouldn't. You won't want to let Mr. Right get away.

Worse yet, if Mr. Right comes along, then makes the terrible mistake of finding someone else, you may think, *I now have to spend the rest of my life either single or with the wrong person.* If that were true, I'd think at the next "heavenly design" meeting you'd have a legitimate gripe. I believe that much of a relationship's timing has to do with God's plan for our growth in him, that a relationship is not *the* plan for our completion, but part of God's plan for our growing in His grace. The sad thing is, often, people who need other people to feel complete or feel okay about themselves, need many relationships—one right after another, or many all at the same time—to feel some sort sense of wholeness only to learn quickly that the feeling is fleeting, only a momentary blip on an otherwise very empty screen.

That said, we need to realize, if we try to find someone to "complete" ourselves before we do the hard work of growing up, maturing, and becoming a whole person in Christ, our pursuit of relationships will likely becomes an effort to find a kind of completeness, something very different than what God has in mind for us. I've seen this in many I've counseled. They'll come to me carrying the effects of several failed relations, perhaps even failed marriages. They'll say with a very sad, far away confusion. "I don't know why I can't seem to ever have a long-term relationship. I date for a few months, even a year, then things don't work out, and I'm alone again. I have two failed marriages already." My first question to them is, "How long have you been able to go without dating someone, without a relationship? How long have you been able to remain single?"

They'll respond, "Two weeks?" They're climbing the walls after a month. You ever meet anyone like that? Take a moment and reflect on that. In the context of someone being mature enough to date God's way—to date with the objective of finding a godly helpmate—what do you think about someone who absolutely needs to be in a relationship to feel whole, feel complete, to feel okay?

You might respond that their standards are low. Clearly, they might be. If they feel the pressure to be closely connected to someone or some-thing, they'll compromise. They'll have relationships with unsuitable people. They want to be wanted. After all, someone's better than no one.

You might see that such a person probably lives an unstable life, one fraught with insecurity and fear. If a person opts to have an available someone want them for a little while, rather than holding out for what may be years for the right person who'll want them for their whole lives, a few things occur. Their lives are filled with uncertainty, frequently punctuated by high drama and hurt, and to minimize all that, those lives are often filled with unhealthy, even dangerous compromise. They may end up giving and giving and giving but getting very little, if anything. Many troll for relationships like that. If they can find someone willing to give, they're willing to take. Their relationships are definitely not based on the mutual long-term benefit each of the participants brings to the relationship.

In the beginning, everybody's accommodating. On the first date, you go to dinner wherever the other wants to go, you see whatever movie the other wants to see. *Mi casa, su casa*. But again, lasting relationships, healthy relationships are not made up of one way giving or accommodating

Of course you give, but you also need to receive to remain healthy so that you continue to be able to give. God created helpmate relationships. What's that mean? Let's say you're helping a friend move. The last item on the truck is a massive refrigerator. It took three husky football players to move that thing into the truck, and now there's only you and your scrawny friend to move it out of the truck. You need the husky footballers back. To your surprise, they drive up in a car at that very minute and help you move that refrigerator. God provided what you needed—the help—to move that thing. But you didn't need all that muscle to be a complete person in Christ. If those guys hadn't showed up, you'd just think God had something else in mind. You wouldn't be less of a person.

So it is with your helpmate. Life with her or him is much easier, more fulfilling, and your journey to the image of Christ is never lonely. But if he or she never comes, you are still all God made you and you can rest assured, your walk with the Lord will be bountiful. God works through other people to supply our needs, just as, sometimes, he provides them himself.

In fact, I suggest there are three institutions God uses to meet our life needs. First, the family we're born into and grow up with—Mom, Dad, brothers, sisters, grandparents, cousins, and so on. Through them, God provides (to most of us) food, shelter, comfort and security, approval, acceptance, and love. Of course, in many of our homes, it didn't work out that way. I understand that. It didn't in mine. But that's not to say the family as our earthly, early provider wasn't God's design. It's there to meet our first basic physical and spiritual needs.

Largely, to the degree our family does an effective job caring for us, it sets the stage for what we look for in other relationships. If we grow up in a home where love and acceptance is distributed based on performance—if we have to do what's expected and acceptable to be loved—then that's the relationships we'll establish in our future. I perform to get your approval, and when it doesn't come, I perform harder and harder. And I expect you to perform, and I don't like you when you don't. And if you don't often enough, don't let the screen door hit you on your way out.

Or our home life might be fear based. Bad performance gets stern consequences – beatings, loss of comforts, definitely loss of affection and acceptance. Relationships that sprout after that sort of upbringing aren't reward oriented at all. I'm an exceptionally nice guy not because I'm afraid you won't like me, but because I'm hoping you won't punish me – withhold emotionally. Those of us from grossly dysfunctional homes, when we reach adulthood, repeat the same systems and functions we learned in our own homes. Of course, there are many variations on this theme, but who we are in our adult relationships largely comes from our families of origin. God gave these institutions for that purpose.

Another institution God provides to meet needs in our life is the body of Christ. This is where, theoretically, we are surrounded by other Christians, other like-minded people. When you look at the people in the Bible who do not have biological families, orphans and widows, for instance, God gives us admonitions about them. "Pure and undefiled religion before God and the Father is this: *to visit orphans and widows in their trouble, and* to keep oneself unspotted from the world" (Jas. 1:27, emphasis mine). And that's not a "Hi, how are you doing?" kind of visit. This is an "assure their safety, care, and well-being" visit. Since they are part of God's family, they are now part of your family too.

God is saying quite pointedly, when one of our own has needs such as hunger, grief, even less acute needs like a leaky faucet, they're struggling in relationships. We have, and are part of, a broader family that is the body of Christ. Our spiritual family can rally around, help, and encourage us. So we have a biological family, and we have a spiritual family.

The third institution is that family you will create one day yourself. Enter the helpmate. Your future husband or wife will be that helpmate not to do the things for you that you're child-hood family wasn't able to do but to help you in that role God's laid out for you. That's why when you get married, you leave your childhood family and "cleave" to your spouse. Your new family relationship becomes primary, and your childhood family moves into the background.

Of course, that's sometimes easier said than done. Even in dating relationships, let alone marriage, parents get in the way. You may have already experienced that. I can't tell you how many women I've counseled who are in competition with another woman. And it's not another girlfriend. It's Mom. Why? Because the guy hasn't matured and constantly seeks Mom's advice. Mom remained the guy's primary source for approval and validation. It's his wife who seems to be the one getting in the way.

Mom's giving counsel, instruction, and direction—all the time. And he habitually goes there, rather than leaving Mom's inter-ference and seeking all that from God and the one who is now his lifemate. This same phenomenon happens between daughters and daddies too. Sometimes, Dads just don't let their daughters grow up. When the nuptials explode upon them, they still want to believe they're still the one man in their little girl's life. That guy she's sleeping with is just an interloper, certainly too young to know what's best for her. Or maybe it's not Dad's fault. It could be the woman is so used to being parented, she's looking for a man to be dad first and husband second, or not at all. And since Dad's given her all she's needed so far, and she's given very little back to him, the relationship with her husband will probably be more of that same—take, take, take—not one that will have the two participants giving what's mutually beneficial.

So again, all those family systems—your childhood family, your spiritual family (the church), and the family you'll build with your helpmate—have to be healthy, practicing healthy boundaries, then work together in order for your adult relationships to last effectively. Again, not just marriage, other relationships are impacted as well.

If we look at this issue under a broader umbrella, it rises to the level of *identity crisis*. The first of which occurred in the garden of Eden. Adam and Eve were created as husband and wife by God and they enjoyed an amazing relationship with their Creator. They had everything they needed and wanted, and what's more, everything was perfect and beautiful. The only thing they couldn't do was eat of the tree of knowledge of good and evil. God forbid it.

Well, in slither's evil, who says, "Hey, how you doing?"

"We're good. We're loved by God. We're happy. We've got everything we need. We're just not ever supposed to eat of this tree."

"Oh, really? Why's that?"

"I don't know. God just said don't eat of this tree because then we'd die. Not a very good thing. It's the tree of the knowledge of good and evil."

"God loves you, right? And education's a good thing. Don't you think he'd want you to have knowledge? You know, I think

43

God's just holding out on you by telling you that you can't eat that fruit on that one tree."

What does she do? She goes against her Creator, the One who had a loving plan for her life and eats the fruit of that tree and hands it to her husband, who does the same. And what does Adam do? The same. And now, we have an identity crisis.

For example, let's think about a handmade watch you may purchase. What if after a few months, it stops keeping time. Where do you go to get it repaired? The manufacturer, right? To the person who made it. And what's the first thing he does? He checks the components to see if it is indeed his handy work and that it has not been altered by another. We are created by God and our true identity is only found in Him. He made us; He knows exactly how we work, and He's placed His mark on us. Every person is created by God's design and our purpose and value come from Him alone.

So when we seek value, purpose, or satisfaction in anything other than the identity we have in Christ, with God the father, we essentially unleash a compulsion to find something else to complete us, rather than completing ourselves in Him. If we're not experiencing a life-giving and sustaining relationship with God and going to Christ for everything we need, we're establishing a void that no one else can fill. No matter how earnestly we seek. There's a lot out there helping us seek it. TV, magazines, movies all tell us we're too fat, too skinny, too dark, too white, have too much hair, have not enough hair, have noses that are too large, or too crooked, have weak abs, and out-of-style glasses. It comes at us at full speed. And if we're not connected to the manufacturer and know He made us just the way He wants us, we're going to believe all the lies we're told. If you're a girl, why wouldn't you believe the first good-looking guy who comes along and tells you that you're beautiful, and you need him to fulfill you sexually? You can see how it comes in and devours us.

But if we're connected to our creator and trust that we have been made to His specifications, then when you think of the family structure He put in place, you trust that too. In the book of Ephesians, for instance, He tells us the husband and father is the structure's roof and walls. He's the protector. Adam forsook that position. He was designed to stop Eve, to rebuke her, but he didn't. He stood there and then let her rebellion become his own. He should have kept what wanted to come through the roof and through the walls out. But he didn't.

Then, while the husband and father is protecting, the wife and mother takes on an incredibly beautiful marital identity, one of support—beautiful, uplifting, upholding column of support smack-dab in the middle of the home. Our culture, though, hates this role for our women. So much of our culture is constructed to rob that identity—that role—and substitute another. Our women should have careers, leaving their homes to babysitters and day-care workers. A career makes a woman whole, not a sound, God-fearing family.

In our Foundations for Lasting Relationships class, students searched the internet for song lyrics that reflect how incomplete we are without being in a relationship. They found expressions such as "I am lost without you," "You make me, me." They all imply that if you haven't had a steady series of "love" relationships by the time you're nineteen or twenty, there's something wrong with you. You, young man or young lady, are seriously lacking. In actuality, you in all probability are far healthier than the person who can't go two weeks without having somebody to hang onto.

Let's talk about something called *enmeshment*. What's that mean? Enmeshment is when people come together in a relationship and lose their spiritual identity as God's Child. They become entangled with another person emotionally and their emotions and life focus is upon them. Spiritual identity becomes a mixture of what they used to be and that with which this new love relationship infuses in them. However, when two whole people who are fully connected to and growing with God, connect and form a meaningful relationship, instead of their focus shifting from the godly, it expands to include the new person. God remains the most important thing in our lives, the most important happening in our lives. The other person becomes somebody who's important and special, but not all consuming.

We can affect one another's lives, and like two people on the dance floor, we move close, then move away; we work together, and then separately, we laugh, we concentrate, we help, we coordinate, all in the context of leading God centered lives. We're still two whole people enjoying one another while our primary focus is still heavenward.

There's energy to all this, and it seems the more we allow the relationship to develop God's way, keeping Him at the center of it, the more energy the relationship has. When it leads to marriage, and the two become one—the two people become one in God's sight, in their way of living and building a family; however, each is individually connected with God. In friendship, we need that same combination of relationship unity and personal connection with God. As God consumes more affection, more thought, more everything in our lives, we can truly experience intimacy with others.

Codependency occurs when this other person begins to occupy that spot in our hearts reserved for God and consumes that which we've previous reserved for God. When that happens, that person has taken the place of Jesus. The song *You Needed Me* springs from this dysfunction. She's lost her identity and the person with whom she's entangled has to leave, so she latches on. If he leaves, her identity leaves with him. He's filled a void, but only for a moment. It's a void that can only be filled by her creator. And the more she tried to force fit some into that void, the more hurt she causes herself.

This is the reason for this book. To help you fill this void as the creator intended with Christ. But there may be a lot working against you, particularly if you emerged from a home where the protector, father, mother, big brother, was an abuser. When we have such a history, we venture into adulthood with an incredibly diverse and effective tool kit that has, up until now, helped us survive. The tool kit's full too, if you grew up in a home where Mom or Dad was super controlling—not teaching or allowing you to make decisions as you matured. The rule of thumb is, the heavier the tool kit, the more damage done to the person trying to carry it along.

One of the goals of this text is to help you develop a biblically based vision of what lasting and healthy relationships look like as in our culture working examples are getting fewer and fewer and fewer. My hope is that it will be this generation who will capture a fresh vision and capacity for lasting relationships. Let's look at other aspects of healthy dependency.

We'll start by looking at two kinds of relationships. The first involves you and someone you're not particularly attracted to. But that someone needs you a lot, won't let you alone, talks in terms of *we* and *us*, and dies the death of a thousand cuts when you fail to ask him or her out. We call those folks *stalkers*. Then there's the relationship where you're really attracted to the other person in some way, their mind, their personality, and the person is attracted to you as well. We call that a *dream*. Those relationships are not the same, right?

In the first relationship, we might excuse that other person's behavior with the statement, "There are people who are just needy." No. We all have needs. In fact, there have been studies and even conclusions that all human beings have needs. Abraham Maslow is credited for developing what's called the hierarchy of human needs.

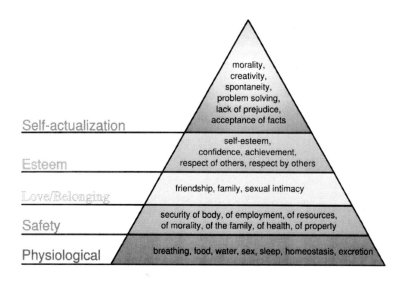

Some of you reading this have studied this already, but for those who haven't, there are fundamental needs at the base such as food and shelter. Then as we climb, there's safety and security. Then certain relationship needs such as friendship, family, intimacy; higher level such approval, affirmation, value. We all need everything on the chart, right? When we say somebody's particularly needy in a relationship, what are we really saying about them? We're saying they aren't able to fulfill their needs on their own, or from those other elements of their lives they've been naturally given, family, for instance. Or they need more of something from you that you don't need from them. Giving between you is disproportionate—draining. And the less we're attracted to that person, the more draining it is.

However, if the other person is somebody we're particularly attracted to, then when they need us, it doesn't feel the same way, does it? Why is that? I think when we're in a healthy, give-and-take relationship, we're balanced. We have our needs being met as we meet the other person's. Then, when they do need a disproportionate serving, we're willing to give it. Probably because we know if we get into a needy situation, the other person will step up to the plate and do his or her part. In a healthy relationship, God completes us; the other person is just part of that provision.

Our focus then, as we grow and mature, should not be trying to find a person to complete us and meet all our needs, but rather to become a person that is sufficient under God. The key here is the term *sufficient under God*. You can be sufficient on your own and attribute it to God. When you're totally self-sufficient you need no one else—nobody, no time, nowhere, nothing. No one wants to have a long-term relationship with anyone to whom there's nothing to give. There's something very intimate about being able to give. If they need nothing you can provide, you begin to believe you have no place, no value in the relationship, which you don't.

I attended a conference many years ago as a single adult. I met a man who asked me to list the ten characteristics I wanted in my wife, my lifemate. I was being asked to draw a target. This is okay to do. This is why football coaches will get together between games and dispassionately decide what they'll have the team do in certain on-field, game situations. It takes the passion of the moment out of it, so the decisions are well thought out. There may be a great deal of passion and emotion in meeting "the right" person, so stepping back to gather perspective can be a good thing.

But let me tell you a better thing. Make a list of attributes *you* want to possess when the time comes to choose a mate. For instance, you want to be financially responsible, comfortable in your own skin, have a strong relationship with God through Christ, well thought of at work, able to put together a responsible set of priorities, and stick to them. Maybe you could add of a few more to the list.

The focus becomes *being* a certain person instead of *finding* a certain person. Let's consider that according to a report published by UNICEF in India, 90 percent of marriages are formulated through arrangement. About 90 percent of the families still begin with parents choosing who their son or daughter will marry. I'm not sure we'd like that "arrangement." We like to choose our own mates. We think by choosing our own our satisfaction with our marriage will be high, and the chance that we'll divorce will be low. We know best, right?

I had the privilege of having an eight-and-a-half-hour train ride across India with a sociologist from the University of Delhi.

"If 90 percent of the people in your culture still have marriages arranged by their parents, what's your divorce rate?" I asked.

"Our divorce rate is in the teens actually, less than 20 percent ever divorce."

"But what about satisfaction? Staying together is one thing, but are people satisfied with their marriages? Are they happy?"

"Our culture has a high level of satisfaction with people who stay married."

I was perplexed by his answer, but then I realized, as a Christian, we believe our marriages have all been arranged, not by our earthly parents but by our heavenly Father. He's chosen somebody for you. And He'll bring that person when the time is right.

We all believe that, right? And if we believe our Heavenly Father will do for us as He did for Adam, he has created a life-mate for you. Then do you think that he just has your interests in mind? If he's going to create a dream person for you, show His concern for your well-being, demonstrate His care for you, His nurture, support, and encouragement, He'll provide through the lifetime mate He's created for you. Or do you think he's just concerned about you and not the other person?

That said, do you think He's going to bring some stellar Christian mate to you when you're an immature, self-centered, marginal believer? Not likely. Why would He inflict that kind of person on someone who has demonstrated an unfailing love for Him through the life he or she leads? What you want to do is rise spiritually to the level you want your mate to have risen to. If you want a mature mate, rise to the level of maturity. If you want a loving, giving mate, rise to the level of being loving and giving. If you want a mate who is committed to your happiness, rise to the level of a saint who will be committed to your mate's happiness. Rise to the level of the amazing human being you want your mate to have risen to. Then you'll be the kind of person God will want to entrust His amazing child to. The reason you haven't found the amazing man or woman you want is because you aren't the amazing woman or man God wants you to be. This might beg the question, "Are you saying there is one right person for me?"

I'm not talking about a person. I'm talking about a type of person. I'm not talking about a particular individual. I'm talking about the characteristics the person should have. He or she should be mature, capable of providing what a mate should. He or she should be less self-centered, be spiritually minded, and secure in their relationship with God—be faithful. That's a type of person. Now the particular person (?)—Bill, Carol, Cindy, or Tom (?)—that's for time and God to reveal to us.

Is it possible for you to marry the wrong person? You might very well marry someone different than who you were looking for. Right now, you should be looking for a person like I just described. But in the throws of the passion or in the midst of an emotional void, you might end up marrying someone very different. Is it the wrong person? No. You're in that marriage and God's nature of grace and mercy can redeem our choices if we live daily trusting Him.

In classes, I have asked, "Does anyone not think the Heavenly Father has someone out there for you?" I'm not pinpointing a particular person. I'm pinpointing the type of person you want God to bring. And if you want God to bring that type of person, you'd better become that type of person God would want that type of person to spend the rest of his or her life with. End of story. Otherwise, you're asking God to essentially unequally yoke two of His children. I believe our good God has both yours and your lifemate's well-being in mind at all times.

It's about being rather than finding. To bring it down to an earthly decision, one many of you guys will be called upon to make sometime in the future. When my daughter got to that dating age, whenever she brought a new guy around, I had to ask myself, "Is this the man that I want my daughter to spend the rest of her life with?" My daughter Gabrielle is an amazing young woman. There are so many beautiful things about her, her heart among them. To me, giving her to some guy is a sacred, sacred thing. And I don't want to entrust someone that precious and valuable to me to just any schmuck who comes along.

Of course, when it comes to my daughter, I don't know if anybody's going to come along I'll feel is a suitable mate. It's because of the value of that relationship. Being equally yoked is being joined with a like-minded individual. The concept comes from the farm. We often understand it to mean being yoked with an unbeliever. I challenge that. The picture is not of two different species. Farmers yoke two of a kind—two oxen, two large cattle, two water buffalo. Not a sheep and a goat or a cat and a dog. Generally speaking, equally yoked is two beasts of burden that are the same species of similar size and similar strength. You don't want two yoked together where one is stronger than the other one. They won't be able to pull evenly together; they'll end up plowing in a circle, getting nowhere.

Which says, being equally yoked is not just about the other person being a Christian. I know he's been baptized in a beautiful service, and he's a member of the church, even goes sometimes. The question is, is he or she active? Is he or she a follower of and spiritually growing in Christ. Does he or she have the maturity to be seriously reminded so their life is not self-centered and he or she can give of themselves to others, specifically hold up their part of the bargain when you and he or she become one?

In a few chapters, we'll look at the attributes of that maturity. We'll discuss how you recognize it, how it might differ between men and women. For women, what are you to look for in a man's life that show he's grown enough and has matured enough to be a lifemate to anyone.

For men, what should a man look for in a woman's life that shows she's developed enough spiritually and mature enough emotionally that she can be a good helper and lifemate to any man, not just you. It's about who she is in Christ, not necessarily what she can do for us. If we can't balance a checkbook, should our lifemate be able to? If we like to golf, should our lifemate golf? It could be a no to both of those questions. The focus is not about finding things in common, or things she can do that I can't. Rather, we need to look at where we are spiritually and in our walk with Christ and allow God to bring the person who will complement our strengths and weaknesses.

I met and then dated Roxanna for a year but then we separated. More than two years passed before we dated again and eventually married. When we looked back, the reason we split up is because we weren't at our points of maturity and spiritual completion that would allow for our relationship to last.

College students have asked me for twenty-five years, "How do you know when you've found the right one?" That's the age-old question. And the answer isn't about finding the right one; it's about being the right one. Roxanna and I didn't have a checklist, and if we had, neither of us would have fulfilled it.

I also know a girl who grew up in the home of an incredibly God-fearing minister. Her parents prayed all her life that the man she would marry would be a virgin. That was one of the elements on the parents' checklist. Well, along comes Steve, a God-fearing, Jesus-loving, and passionate man, but he wasn't a virgin. He came to Christ out of worldly self-serving existence. But he was now a godly man. He did not fit the checklist. But God has blessed that marriage and that family abundantly. Now if the checklist had prevailed, the whole family—parents and the children—would have missed out on that blessing. But of course, it didn't. God's plans trump the will of men (and women).

Since "finding" your lifemate is about *being* rather than *finding*, timing matters. I was once asked, "Do you think the guy I am now dating is the kind of person I could spend the rest of my life with?" And my answer was, "Not right now." I'd look at the guy's life and see some maturity and some demonstrated immaturity. He could grow and mature to become lifemate material someday, but he's not there yet. He may very well be the right guy, but he needs more time and a longer walk with God before he will be ready to take on the roles of husband, father, and spiritual leader of a family.

I perform premarital counseling for many couples. Sometimes, as part of the counseling process, I administer diagnostic tests revealing big issues that need to be worked through. When it happens, I advise them not to marry right now. "Just push the date back a little and then take that time to grow and learn to care for and meet one another's needs." When the couple focuses on maturing and growing, it's amazing how their lives can change, and when they do, their relationship gets healthier and their future truly brightens.

Being honest about these issues is a matter of transparency, which will be discussed in chapter 7. If you are going to seriously date someone, and if the person is on the short list of possible lifemates, you need to be honest about elements of your life that will be relationship issues. If you have habits, hang-ups, those sorts of issues that impact your relationships, you need to be up front about them. All of us, to some degree or another, have issues we bring to relationships. Perhaps you've been badly hurt in some way and have some suppressed anger about it, you have certain fears that you're dealing with, fears or anger that affect your close relationships. We need to be transparent with those who are investing their emotions in us.

We need to be direct in developing relationships and ask questions such as "What have been some of the struggles that you have experiences in past relationships?" or "What's the longest time you have gone without being in a relationship?" If the answer is fourteen days, it's a flag, a flag revealed through direct inquiry.

Honesty within your relationship allow each of you to understand the hazards that may be lurking. You also need to be discerning. No one intentionally writes on E-Harmony that they're looking for someone to meet all their needs. "I want someone to fulfill me from the inside out and someone to make me whole.

And I want him to put me on a pedestal to be treated like a princess." Even though they don't write it out in so many words, that may be what they do want. You need to ask the direct questions and listen to their answers to discern their capacity for lasting and health relationships

I was counseling a couple a few months ago; they've been married ten years and have three children. She told me, "When my husband, Jerry, is happy, the world is fine. When Jerry's not happy, my world and my children's world is hell." The cause of the problem—their relationship is characterized by Jerry's all-consuming need to be in control and have his needs met 24/7. In their ten years of marriage, nothing had changed. Now, she has to keep things happy for Jerry, for her sake, and the sake of her children, because life's not good around the house when Jerry's not happy. She added, "I knew he was a big baby when we dated and even when we first married, but I thought he would have grown up by now."

PRACTICING FORGIVENESS

There is nothing that happens in a relationship—absolutely nothing that can't be forgiven through the perfect work of Jesus Christ on the cross. That event in world history is the line in the sand for all of us. We are often too proud to receive this forgiveness for ourselves, making it impossible to offer it to someone else. Forgiveness flows through us to others if we have received it and as we receive it. We don't make it or give it on our own.

Building a relationship without a biblical understanding of forgiveness will only lead to unnecessary hurt, resentment, and bitterness. Easier said than done, but I'm here to tell you now, no relationship will last without it. Relationships do not exist without hurt, offense, and sin.

Forgiveness is the application of the cross to someone else for whom Jesus died. This is where we must begin. Once we set our mind upon the truth of grace housed in the payment of Jesus's perfect blood atonement, then we are in a position to give permission to the Holy Spirit to help us in our will to release the other person from our condemnation and punishment. As we surrender to this way of the soul, our emotions, through the Spirit comforter's help, will be free to reposition and appropriate feelings will possibly come to pass. This is not always the same as reconciliation, but reconciliation is not possible without true remedy for sin being applied to the situation first. We will deal with reconciliation at a later point in this chapter. Forgiveness, which must occur before reconciliation, is the act of relinquishing all claims you think you might have on someone for retribution, revenge, and any negative behavior toward the person. Our entire soul—the mind, will, and emotions—must be engaged in the forgiveness process.

Think of the worst sin you have ever committed and have felt the most guilt and condemnation over. Get this in your head first. Then recall the scenes in the movie, *The Passion of the Christ.* If you think your sin was (is) so horrible that the agony, pain, suffering, and death that Jesus endured isn't enough, then you are way too proud of your sin. To believe your sin is so great even Jesus's sacrifice is not enough to cover it is to believe your sin is too great. This is pride. Pride will keep you from receiving forgiveness, and pride will keep you from forgiving. Pride destroys relationships.

Therefore, if we don't forgive and continue in our pride and stubbornness, which we all have been known to do unless we repent and have a complete change of disposition, then the relationship will be set up perfectly for repeated offenses and resentments. Forgiveness doesn't have a Reserved For label. It is necessary and applicable to any given time, place, offense, violation with any situation or group of people.

If it's so important, then we need to make it a fact of our lives. But how do we do that? Probably the best place to start our journey is with the big wrongs that have been done to us. Wrongs that have really hurt, maybe even scarred us, wrongs that haunt us every day and color every one of our relationships with shadowy tinges of gloom and dread and anger.

You ask, "Release all claims to getting even, getting a satisfaction? You've got to be kidding. Just let him/her get away with it? No retribution?" I know what you're thinking. You're thinking it's not fair what happened to you, what they did to you. You are thinking it would be a sin to let them off the hook. After all, doesn't God think I am valuable?

The answer is yes. You are valuable. You are so valuable that He forgives you but also loves you too much to let you live with the burden of being the judge, jury, and the equalizer for all wrongs done against you. You are too valuable to let you go on thinking your form of justice is better and more exacting than a holy God. But no, it would not be a sin to let them off the hook. Stay with it. Keep reading.

Too many people think forgiveness and reconciliation are the same thing. Forgiveness is not the same as reconciliation. They are not. We release people through the perfect work of Jesus, but that doesn't mean we cozy up again as though nothing ever occurred. There is a sweet companion to forgiveness. It is called grief. The Bible calls it sorrow. The following is a testimony about forgiveness from my wife, Roxanna.

> I was deeply offended by a very close friend when my daughter was in middle school. It involved my daughter finding out about an earlier godless event in my life that was extremely destructive and painful. She found out I had an abortion. I had not decided to never tell her. I just simply had not been led by God to tell her at that point. Upon finding out in a way that was not God's plan, it was put upon her to have to process some very devastating things about her mom before she was spiritually and emotionally developed.
>
> Upon her birth, the Lord began a healing and forgiveness journey in me. I was able to allow myself to receive the love and forgiveness of God, love and name my aborted baby in heaven, and finally forgive myself. So, when I didn't get to be the first and only one to share the story I felt totally robbed of being able to testify of the Lord's grace, love, and forgiveness. It would have been more protective over the gate that had been swung open in her heart, making it easy for the devil to get a foothold. She had an added layer to deal with. It's enough to find out there was a lost sibling and a mother with a past, but to deal with the betrayal of finding out the way she did was more than she could bear up on her own, especially

at her age. I needed to forgive the person for telling her, and I needed to forgive God for allowing it, and myself for possibly missing God's instructions to me to tell her. And painfully wait for my daughter to forgive me and struggle with God in her own right to get out from under the pain of living with unforgiveness toward her betrayer.

The point of forgiveness for the person who told her came at a very distinct moment and serves as the centerpoint in all that needs forgiven in my life since that day. I was at a worship event at a University where Jamie Smith was leading us in a prayer night for the nations. We were singing that old song, When I Survey the Wondrous Cross. Our betrayer at the time was sitting four rows ahead of me—8 months pregnant, and my daughter was sitting beside me. We got to the words,

> "See from his head, his hands, his feet,
> Where love and sorrow flow mingling down."

I was stopped in that moment and I physically and spiritually felt the truth and peace of the Lord Jesus Christ flood in. In fresh brokenness I just stood there. His holiness, power, purity and love began pouring into my spirit. In that God ordained moment, the Spirit spoke of Jesus' grief with me when He was betrayed and that He understands my sorrow over this betrayal. Although it pales in comparison, the Holy Spirit revealed nothing of a minimizing nature.

I realized my sin and unwillingness to forgive up until this point was out of a fear that God was minimizing my pain and especially the pain and suffering of my daughter. But the words to the song were telling me something different. Love and sorrow (grief) co-exist. His punishment and suffering for my sin and my betrayers were forgiven, and at the same time He does not minimize our pain, He was taking it in our place. He loves me. He loves the betrayer and He loves my daughter. His love offers the forgiveness, but His sorrow tells me even though it is forgiven, He knows the grief in my heart. In short, He acknowledged the pain at the same time He enabled me to release my betrayer.

I quickly moved four rows ahead, embraced her, and told her "it is finished. It is covered." I held her for a moment while we both wept, her pregnant belly protruding into my gut where I knew He also felt that loss so long ago, and paid for my ultimate betrayal. I was done being the victim of her betrayal and let all the grace and perfect remedy apply to my view of her. My disposition changed immediately; the reconciliation came over time and by the power of His Spirit.

Satan hates forgiveness. It is like a weapon against his cunning strategies to pit us against one another and keep us from stepping into His grace and favor over our relationships.

My sweet daughter walked her own path to forgiving our betrayer. She came to forgive me as well as her. One year later the three of us did the "Walk for Life" together as we took turns pushing the stroller for her one year old-the child she was pregnant with at the time of the betrayal.

Forgiveness is commanded. While we choose it- we are simply stepping into and participating in what only God can do. Reconciliation with those who sin against us is not always commanded. We are always commanded to commit the ultimate reconciliation to God as it counts for eternity. But forgiveness can lead to earthly reconciliation.

—Roxanna Grimes

Forgiveness, Affairs, and Divorce

We cannot deal with biblical forgiveness in relationships without taking a look at what the Bible says about forgiveness and sex outside God's design. Let's start by looking at a passage where Jesus addresses this very issue: Matthew 19:9, "And I say unto you, Whoever shall put away his wife, except it be for fornication, and shall marry another commits adultery: and who marries her which is put away doth commit adultery" (KJV). We're told here that one of the only grounds for divorce is adultery. If you're in a marriage relationship and your spouse betrays you with another, you are free in God's eyes to leave. It's a grievous breach—vows have been broken, hearts betrayed, trust shattered.

But are you commanded to leave, to divorce? I have folks come into my counseling office from time to time who say, "I found out my wife's been cheating on me. But she's repentant and is truly sorry. She's asked for my forgiveness and wants to save our marriage. But I have no choice, I have to divorce her." Not so! God is a God of reconciliation. It's like some people want a pastor-counselor to punch their "get out of marriage free" card! When He brings two people together, particularly people He knows and love, He hates divorce. If that's true, why did He allow divorce to occur so freely in the Old Testament times?

Jesus answered this question in the previous verse, Matthew 19:8, "Jesus replied, 'Moses permitted you to divorce your wives because your hearts were hard. But it was not this way from the beginning'" (NIV). From the moment we were created in the beginning, we were created man and (a little later) wife. It was a permanent relationship. But after the fall, when our hearts were a couple degrees more pliable than stone, God permitted divorce because we would have sinned even more grievously had we not been able to. But now, our hearts are indwelled with the Holy Spirit; now, our hearts have been reborn; and now, we are able to glory in the way marriage was created to be. Although God permits us to take on divorce, we don't have to. We can choose to forgive and rebuild. This truth extends not only to marriage, but also to dating.

Sexual immorality comes in many forms, particularly in dating. Let's say you're dating a guy and you've make it quite clear that you are determined to remain pure for marriage. No sex, no forms of sexual gratification. Yet the guy you are dating begins to pressure you. You like him and really don't want to lose what you have, but dates are beginning to resemble wrestling matches, and the emotional blackmail is getting pretty black. Let's take it a step further—date rape. Maybe alcohol was involved, maybe just heavy intimidation. The sense of violation is monstrous as is the person doing the violating. You are the victim. "Forgiveness? How? I'll hate him 'til I die." And you'll carry that hate 'til you die as well. And you will have offended your beloved Savior 'til you die. No. God has commanded us to forgive as hard as it is. This is a good example of forgiveness where reconciliation is not only unlikely, but also unholy. We must not return to a relationship that puts us in danger or harm.

When it comes to forgiving sexual sins, the single life is far from immune. That's why God wrote 1 Corinthians 6:18–20. It says something pretty unique. "Flee from sexual immorality. All other sins a person commits are outside the body, but whoever sins sexually, sins against their own body. Do you not know that your bodies are temples of the Holy Spirit, who is in you, whom you have received from God? You are not your own; you were bought at a price. Therefore honor God with your bodies" (NIV).

Flee from sexual immorality. Run away from it like the wind. At the first sign, disappear. Why? Because it's a sin against your own body, the very temple of the Holy Spirit. God the Holy Spirit is making your heart His home, and you are fouling the place. Not only has He taken up residence, but He's bought the place. He's now got the title—you are His. You're fouling up His place, God's place, and God does not dwell in filth. God forgives all sin, but sexual sins have a way of imparting unwanted consequences, such as an unplanned pregnancy. These days, just about everybody knows someone or a family member who wasn't planning to have a child but sex outside of God's design changed all that. Now, even though God will forgive, parents will forgive, boyfriends and girlfriends can forgive, but the consequence lives on.

What about sexually transmitted diseases (STDs)? One of them has devastated a whole continent—AIDS in Africa and in the US, an entire generation. When people who are promiscuous leave the safety God has prescribed for sexual activity—the monogamous marriage relationship—and venture into a world directed by passion there can be bleak consequences. No wonder God wants us to just flee from it. But as with all sin, God forgives sexual sin. You can even forgive yourself, but if you contract a sexually transmitted disease, particularly one that keeps on giving, you still live with the consequences. Which is why, I believe, God labels sexual sins as different.

I can't think of any other sin that carries consequences like these. And these aren't minor consequences, such as petty theft and having to make restitution or lying to someone and losing a little trust. Now you're faced with taking responsibility for raising a child or carrying a disease around for the rest of your life that will affect you, maybe kill you, but that also carries the risk along with it of infecting others, even a trusting spouse. In relationships, these are big, tough issues.

So, sexual sins in the context of marriage, sexual relationships, and divorce are unique from other sins because of their identification in 1 Corinthians 6:18–20. Secondly, sexual sins that victimize marriage are unique because, unlike any other relationship, marriage involves public vows made before God and at least one witness, or a whole auditorium full of them, even a whole church congregation. What other sin has such a launching pad. Stealing? Do you ever stand in church and promise before God and the congregation that you will not steal. How about for covetousness? Or bearing false witness? We can step down the whole list of commandments and the only one we find that requires a public commitment is our vow to love and to be true to someone. We vow to stay together till death, in good times and bad, adversity and prosperity, sickness and health until "death do us part."

Trust Is at the Core

Trust is at the core of all lasting relationships. You can lose trust for your mate even though he or she has only been involved with someone else emotionally, and not physically. Secrecy is what turns a simple friendship with someone other than your mate into a relationship that, even though platonic, threatens your marriage. Trust is open and honest. If there's anything going on you need to hide—e-mails, private notes, secret meetings, voice and text messages. If you need to enforce a password on your computer or listen to your voice mails somewhere alone and delete them immediately because someone might overhear, then your heart is straying from where it should be—infidelity is not limited to sexual betrayal. "But I tell you that anyone who looks at a woman lustfully has already committed adultery with her in his heart" (Matt. 5:28, NIV). If you continue, trust will be breached; confidence in you will be lost. You have vowed before God and perhaps an entire congregation that you're going to stick it out, that you're in it for the long haul, that your relationship will last until one of you stands in tears by the other's grave, but here you are where you shouldn't be. If any of this is true of your relationship, drop to your knees, ask God's forgiveness, and get your focus back to your marriage. It's time to flee.

Another huge impact of divorce that often doesn't accompany other sins is the financial impact of not seeking forgiveness and restoration. In divorce, participants incur the cost of living in separate homes dividing in half family resources. I've been in collegiate teaching and ministry for over twenty years, and I can't tell you how many students I've met who struggle financially because Mom and Dad divorced. But the financial toll is only half of it; the emotional impact is huge. The parents at odds with one another, dividing holidays, trying to get a decision on a big issue (such as overseas travel for school), and there may be residual guilt coming into play. These are stormy seas that need navigational skills we're definitely not born with. The bottom line: divorces rarely serves what is best for the kids. Some can hardly wait for the kids to hit the magic age of eighteen when child support ends. In a divorce, kids can go from a gift from God to be cherished and encouraged, to burdens, and none of us want to be burdens.

In this day and age one of the greatest financial burdens is the cost of a college education. Divorce often makes college impossible or a financial nightmare—huge student loans, working full-time while carrying full academic loads. Not pretty. And it's not just college. I did a wedding recently for a lovely couple, former students, I've known several years. When it came to planning this one day, this day that was supposed to be the happiest day of their lives, they were saddled with all sorts of extra financial and emotional baggage because one set of parents had been divorced. They had to negotiate finances with one parent and then the other. The guest list was an issue. The mother had an army she wanted to invite, the father had but a few, but the parents insisted that each authorized number had to be the same. The day became a struggle of wills instead of a day when two loving families assemble to commemorate a truly blessed event. And the bride and groom had to eat a good deal of the cost—money they could have used to start their life together. Divorce costs everyone a lot.

But the greatest toll, in my view, is divorce is just plain heartbreaking for everyone. It certainly is for me, and I'm just a bystander—all I ever plan to be. For instance, to watch a young bride walk down the aisle without her father is heartbreaking. To watch two people who've vowed to become one flesh battling to the death over who gets the dog is heartbreaking, especially when their young child stands nearby in tears. To watch bright futures obliterated and replaced by anxious uncertainty is heartbreaking. To see a child alone because Mom now has to work is heartbreaking. Seeing a child raised by strangers is heartbreaking. And the list goes on. Broken trust, constant hurt, corroding guilt—all are heartbreaking.

And what about the young mom whose looking into her first child's baby eyes for the first time? A joyous occasion, right? Beyond joyous—euphoric. My life was forever changed the day my firstborn came into the world. Now add to that beautiful moment a bitter, divorced mom and a prideful, antagonistic father who are the grandparents. And put them in that hospital room together. It goes beyond awkward into punitive. Some of you have already been there. You might as well bathe your newborn in arsenic. God's design for family has been marinated in poison, and now, this baby goes home to a toxic family system. I've met and counseled far too many people who grew up in that and are now stunted in God's intimacy design, simply unable to connect and form life lasting bonds. The step design of blended families removes the attachment process one person away from the child, further serving to dwarf their developing ability to connect. All this missing attachment leaves the door open for future violation and abuse, because that's what our enemy, Satan, strategically seeks to do. Find an open door, slip in, and start to destroy from the inside out.

Then later on, stepmom wants to be a grandma. But the kids and the grandkids' parents rebel because "you're not my mother. And you're definitely not their grandmother." And there are other squabbles that rear up to throw you as well. Unless there is forgiveness for all the wrongs—parents, grandparents, siblings, anyone involved in the divorce is on the top of your list—divorce is the gift that keeps on giving all the way to the grave.

Just to put an even sharper point on it, a gentleman in our church went to be with the Lord. A few months later, his son passed away. And because of a broken marriage and corroded relationships on both sides, their battle has spilled into courts. But what makes the emotional and spiritual brutality of it all so sad when it came to attending memorial services for father and son, a child would not attend the service to honor and bury his father because a stepmother would be in attendance. Divorce is truly a tragic pain that keeps on giving.

Whatever tears at your marriage and there are many worldly and satanic claws out there doing just that, when marital infidelity is one of them, drop to your knees and take the need to forgive to the Lord. Call out to Him for the strength, courage, and humility to place it on the cross, to be reconciled through that perfect work once and for all. The consequences of not attempting forgiveness are very great indeed.

It is not easy to forgive. A man from San Diego had his twenty-two-year-old son temporarily living with him. A bright young man, he'd just graduated from college and was camping at Dad's place until he could find a job. One morning, the boy decided to run over to the corner grocery store to pick up some things, and on the way there, he got caught in the crossfire between two rival gangs and was killed. The dad was devastated. His heart was ripped out of him that morning. The gangbanger who did it was caught and brought to trial. During the trial, Dad attended. From the moment he stepped into that courtroom and saw the lowlife who had murdered his son, he was consumed by hate. He wanted to do to that boy what that boy had done to his. But being a Christian, he knew he had to forgive. And so he started praying and praying, and there were days when he thought he was close. What made forgiveness even more difficult was as he sat in the spectator section or the courtroom, the killer would look at him, taunt him, and mouth how satisfying it had been to kill Dad's son. But the Christian man knew what God commanded, and he also knew the destruction hate was doing to him. And so, over time, he forgave. He gave his claim to the ultimate equalizer, the Lord Jesus Christ, through His perfect work on the cross that was enough even for this horror. Every now and again, he has to revisit the issue, particularly when someone says to him, "I'll see you in a few minutes," because those were the last words his son said to him. Each time he hears those words, he must apply the perfect remedy to his loss again. Forgiveness can be a monumental task, one only God can facilitate. Don't hesitate to get to your knees in worship and surrender the situation in the perfect remedy of His blood poured out over it—immediately after you've been wronged.

A dear friend of Rox's recently lost her grandson to suicide. Suicide is so painful because it involves an extra layer of grief of someone choosing to leave our life permanently through death. Having a lifestyle of intimacy with Jesus, one of her first statements to Rox after the initial heartbreak and shock was, "The Lord has me tucked up under His wing, and I am seeing feathers." The only place our hearts are prepared for releasing people in forgiveness is in abiding close to Him.

To get back to divorce, one reason I have such strong convictions about this issue is this: I believe the Bible teaches; even in the case of adultery in marriage, divorce is permitted but not commanded. And the consequences of forgiveness can be all positive, while the consequences for not forgiving can be a train wreck for everyone.

Even the language of scripture is on the side of forgiveness and reconciliation. When the Pharisees confronted Jesus and claimed Moses commanded divorce, Jesus said, "No. Moses permitted divorce because people's hearts were hard." Divorce was permitted because the people were excellent sinners. But now that God has softened the heart and taken up residence, He's there to keep the family together.

So far we've talked about forgiveness generally, but there are different types of forgiveness.

Three Types of Forgiveness

Governmental forgiveness is that when forgiveness occurs, consequences may remain. Psalms 32 gives us a good look at what God's forgiveness means.

Blessed is the one
whose transgressions are forgiven,
whose sins are covered.
Blessed is the one
whose sin the LORD does not count against them
and in whose spirit is no deceit.

Psalm 32:1–2 (NIV)

A primary example of governmental forgiveness can be seen in substance abuse. The temporal consequences may include children. Kids from "alcoholic" homes can carry emotional baggage all the way into the assisted living years. Infants of alcoholic mothers may be born with Fetal Alcohol Syndrome. An abuser may have gotten a DUI—very inconvenient, expensive, and is guaranteed to come back and haunt. Or while driving, the alcoholic may have been involved in an accident and taken someone's life. You may be forgiven but that's far from the end of it.

Another example is the consequence of promiscuity. For example, if you get an STD. You may have experienced forgiveness from God, others, and self. But you may carry the disease into your future. In fact, into every relationship you'll have from them on. I can't tell you the number of times I've counseled students who have now fallen in love, now met the person they want to spend life with, want only to honor and support them, certainly don't want to rock the boat in anyway, but need to not only confess to a sexual past, but tell their new love that sexual past is going to be brought into their marriage so much so, in fact, that the loved one may end up affected for life as well.

But isn't the past just the past and there's really no need for the conversation? You should have it, even if an STD isn't involved. I'm counseling a couple in their late twenties. He was not honest with her about his sexual past. Now married with a child, she learned about his previous sexual escapades. They're down the road pretty far, and it's not going well for them. A major contribution to her negative feelings for him center on her belief that he lied to her by not disclosing his past. "How do I know you're telling me the truth, even now?" It's a point hard for him to argue. We're going to have a long talk about forgiveness, but trust and forgiveness are two different things, as are forgiveness and respect and forgiveness and love. She may release him in forgiveness but the effects of it may linger for this guy for a long, long time.

Pure before God, Even in Consequences

When we're forgiven, at any level, we are pure before God based on His remedy through the cross event; we're pure in His sight.

But more than that, "Now if we are children, then we are heirs—heirs of God and co-heirs with Christ, if indeed we share in his sufferings in order that we may also share in his glory" Rom. 8:17. We're God's children in every sense of the word—coheirs with His only begotten son. Titus gives the same information this way: "So that, having been justified by his grace, we might become heirs having the hope of eternal life" Titus 3:7.

Even as children of God, joint heirs with Christ, pure in the sight of God, totally forgiven, we will often suffer the consequences of our sin. The example previously mentioned is Fetal Alcohol Syndrome. If the mother abuses alcohol, even if she comes to know the Lord before the baby is born, her child may be born with this syndrome and experience the following:

- Poor growth while the baby is in the womb and after birth
- Decreased muscle tone and poor coordination
- Delayed development and problems in three or more major areas—thinking, speech, movement, or social skills
- Heart defects such as ventricular septal defect (VSD) or atrial septal defect (ASD)
- Problems with the face, including:

  - narrow, small eyes with large skin folds
  - small head

- small upper jaw
- smooth groove in upper lip
- smooth and thin upper lip

Forgiveness doesn't mean consequences evaporate. It just means we stand clean before God and are now capable of a close and intimate relationship with others.

Eternal Forgiveness. Now let's discuss eternal forgiveness. This forgiveness focuses on our relationship with God and eternity and on what scripture prescribes so that we might live with God in and for eternity. To sum up all Scripture on the subject, we simply have to deal with our sinful nature and our sinful choices—past, present, and future—piece a cake, right? Actually, in one sense, it is. Let's take a look at this most important subject.

Romans 3:10–18 (NIV) gives us a thorough look at man's spiritual state before God:

> There is no one righteous, not even one; there is no one who understands; there is no one who seeks God. All have turned away, they have together become worthless; there is no one who does good, not even one.
> Their throats are open graves; their tongues practice deceit.
> The poison of vipers is on their lips.
> Their mouths are full of cursing and bitterness.
> Their feet are swift to shed blood; ruin and misery mark their ways, and the way of peace they do not know."
> There is no fear of God before their eyes.

Then Romans 3:23, sums it up when it tells us, "All have sinned and fall short of the glory of God." Okay, so what? We're not perfect. Who is? Is God really so petty He will hold a few little infractions against me?

God's not petty. God is righteous and just. He cannot allow sin or rebellion against Him to go unpunished. And so we're told in Romans 6:23, "For the wages of sin is death." We sin, we die—eternally. So how then are we saved for this inevitable end? Romans 6:23 goes on to say, "But the gift of God is eternal life in Christ Jesus our Lord." When we have God's gift of grace and his gift of mercy credited to us in salvation, the word is *imputed*. How then does this "imputation" take place? Romans 10:9 tells us, "If you declare with your mouth, "Jesus is Lord," and believe in your heart that God raised him from the dead, you will be saved." And Christ's righteousness will be imputed to you. At that instant, we enter into a relationship with God the Father as His child. But what about all this talk about eternity? Have you ever known a relationship that lasts forever? Well, hear about this one. This is a secure relationship, and it lasts eternally. As Romans 8:38–39 puts it, "For I am convinced that neither death nor life, neither angels nor demons, neither the present nor the future, nor any powers, neither height nor depth, nor anything else in all creation, will be able to separate us from the love of God that is in Christ Jesus our Lord" (NIV). This is eternal forgiveness, now and into our next life with Him in heaven.

Temporal Forgiveness. The final type of forgiveness is temporal forgiveness. Temporal forgiveness concerns our daily walk. "Forgive our debts and we forgive our debtors." It generally doesn't include catastrophic events, such as eternity, or the consequences of governmental forgiveness. Temporal forgiveness fall under the heading of those sins John confronts in 1 John 1:9 (NIV), "If we confess our sins, he is faithful and just and will forgive us our sins and purify us from all unrighteousness." It's asking God daily for forgiveness for our daily sin that transgress against Him. It's relationship maintenance. It's remaining humble before our Maker. It's keeping our place before a righteous God in the forefront of our minds. For example, Matthew 5:23–24 offers this admonition: "Therefore, if you are offering your gift at the altar and there remember that your brother or sister has something against you, leave your gift there in front of the altar. First go and be reconciled to them; then come and offer your gift"(NIV). It's not good for us to be at odds with our Christian brother or sister. We go to God, ask forgiveness for the part we might have had in the relationship breach, and then we go make amends and walk with God in gratitude for having been made clean.

Or you wake up and, other than the English exam that's coming up that morning, you have only one other thing on your mind—the two pop tarts waiting for you in the fridge. You head for the kitchen. The pop tarts are gone. Your roommate's eaten them. You even see residual crumbs near the toaster. He didn't even ask. He just purloined the pop tarts and headed off leaving you the crumbs. That guy will never eat pop tarts in this town again!

It's not catastrophic, right? Pop tarts aren't human beings. There's nothing governmental about it—the lasting effects are minimal. It's just not a big thing. But little things can matter, when friends disregard your feelings or your property. We get offended and hurt. "Do I mean that little to them? Am I invisible or don't I exist?" And little things can fester, create sores that, if untreated, grow and blister with poison. The treatment, of course, is temporal forgiveness. You give it over to the Lord, harbor no desire for revenge, you leave the guy's Twinkies absolutely alone, and you move on. If losing your pop tarts is a big relationship issue for you, lock them up next time.

Now that we've identified the types of forgiveness, let's take the next step and cover the "how to forgive." How do you find it within yourself to forgive people?

The Three Rs of Forgiveness

Release

If someone takes your pop tarts and you don't care, when he apologizes, you say, "De nada." It's nothing. Don't worry about it. I'm fine. But if you loan your new Honda Civic to the guy and he totals it, that's a bit bigger issue. If you keep toll money and loose change in your ashtray and your buddy runs a bit short and takes a couple bucks without asking, and then you find out about it, you might wave an unconcerned hand and say, "De nada." No biggie. Buy me a burger some time. But if that same guy sneaks into your dorm room and lifts a couple hundred bucks from your savings for next semester's tuition, that's much bigger—a more strident violation of trust, a much bigger deal.

Or if your boyfriend tells you he can't see you this evening because he has to study for a physics test the prof told them about only today, then you find out he wasn't studying at all, but went to a party with some girl in his study group, what then? He lied and he violated your trust, you lost respect, and everything between you is affected.

What I'm trying to point out here is there are degrees of violation. I want you to see that. Living in a connected and intimate relationship with the Lord through the help of the Holy Spirit means that whenever we are violated, no matter how big or small, His existing presence inside us will enable us to see and apply all the remedy to the given situation. We just can't manage to forgive anyone for anything without bringing the presence of God into it. Forgiveness starts with a humble stance before the Lord over our own sinful wanderings. I don't have the ability to release such a violation without God's help. I don't forgive sin. He does. I will let Him, and then I will release them from my sin bent chase to try to get even. Your heart is as black as obsidian at the bottom of a well at midnight. Perhaps you didn't perpetrate the same sin, but you've perpetrated others, and you're certainly capable of not only matching the sin but doing your abuser one better. After all, isn't that want you'd like to do to him? Or her? And God forgave you, sent His Son Jesus to die for that particular sin, and wiped your slate clean.

However, if you don't think you've ever done anything wrong and believe you're the one always being violated, then forgiving people will be a struggle for you. Even for unauthorized pop tart devouring. Release their debt. Forgive. What debt? When someone hurts us, they incur a debt to us and retribution seeks payment of that debt. Forgiveness lets go of it, wipes the slate clean as God wiped your slate clean. Another way to look at it is when you forgive. You give up the right to clean their clock, and instead, you clean their slate. You give up your right to punish your betrayer for what they've done.

Why is it good to give up your right to punish aside from God telling you to? Punishing never satisfies. There's nothing you can do to the offender that will make you even, will bring back what you lost, or fulfill the requirement of rage. Nothing. At the end of your punishing act, you'll be as angry as before, and feel as violated as before. Revenge is insatiable. That's why God tells us this:

> It is mine to avenge; I will repay.
> In due time their foot will slip;
> their day of disaster is near
> and their doom rushes upon them.
>
> Deuteronomy 32:35 (NIV)

By giving the debt to God to collect, we not only release ourselves from all that's negative about holding on to it, but the debt is collected in the perfect, most satisfying way, and since it is God who saves, collection of the debt may even lead to the debtor's salvation. And this is our goal for all those who hurt us.

I have a friend, Noel. About twelve or thirteen years ago, right after Thanksgiving, that time of year when we make the turn toward Christmas, he lost his wife, mother, sister and his three children and his unborn child—all at the same moment—to a drunk driver.

I've never been to a funeral with more coffins lined up, some quite small. Even as a man of God, I had no idea how to approach Noel. What could I possibly say? You see, only God knows what to say; only God has the power to quiet the heart during such turmoil; only God knows how to comfort and soothe. If Noel ignored that fact and if he tried to deal with this huge tragedy himself, what would he do? Run over the guy. Stalk him with an MK-47? Nothing would ever replace Noel's loss, satisfy his rage, or assuage his grief; certainly not while in jail for taking the law into his own hands. Noel's only alternative was to forgive and let the Lord handle it.

Noel did forgive, and surprisingly, the drunk driver survived but had a long stay in the hospital recovering. I find it remarkable that Noel actually visited the guy. It took a while for the Lord to get Noel to that place as you can imagine. And part of God's retribution was that the guy was left unable to walk. But after awhile, the process of forgiveness had Noel go to the man and say, "I choose to release you. I forgive you for killing my family."

Resist

So when you do release your debt to the Lord, what do you do next? What's the next R mean? Resist. Once we release, we must *resist* the sometimes overwhelming desire to take it back. Don't you think after Noel left that man's room, after he told the guy he'd forgiven him, he didn't fight the desire to hurt the guy still? Can't you just hear his head telling him, "You're just going to let that guy go, just let him walk away with having taken everything away from you? How can you do that?" Yes, after we forgive, we still struggle with taking back the debt. "God, I want to avenge. I want to make him suffer." We have to resist with everything we have, and everything is our relationship with a loving, under-standing, comforting God. "God, take this anger from me, and the debt it fills. Yes, I forgave him, but today I'm still angry, still very angry."

Recycle

Complete forgiveness takes time, and it's also going to take the next R—recycling. You must go through the process again and again. It's not a one-time journey. We're not like God. We do not have the capacity to forgive and then forget. Especially those catastrophic types of offenses that alter the courses of our entire lives. God forgives us once and remembers our sin no more. Psalm 103:12 (NIV) describes God's forgiveness of us this way: "As far as the east is from the west, so far has he removed our transgressions from us."

How far is that? If you start driving east, will you ever stop driving east? And if you start driving west, will you ever stop driving west? No. It's God's way of saying He removes them an infinite distance—to a place beyond all others. Only God can forgive and remember our sin no more. Only God.

But for us, we can throw nothing further than our memory. And that's the rub. We can struggle, we can toil, we can cry out to God for help, we can cry out to others. We can go through counseling and deliverances processes, and still, because of our imperfect earthly existence, we'll remember. And the rage comes flooding back. The enemy will use the past to bait you and trip you up sending you reeling like a fish on the end of a hook. And so you recycle—clear in the knowledge that to release and resist are choices you make. God empowers you. And ultimately, it serves His good purposes, and you walk in freedom over that—again. To release it is to release the bondage in which the violation has caught you, and it will no longer bear its power over you.

Here's another story of forgiveness. Another friend, Dan, grew up without a father. His dad abandoned his mother when he was three years old, just a little guy. Fast forward fifty-four years. Dan's now fifty-seven. In that time, he's never heard from his dad, doesn't even know if his dad is still alive. Then one day, he learns from a cousin that not only is his father still alive, but he lives only one hundred miles away. For fifty-four years, Dan carried the bitterness to being deserted and then ignored. "Why didn't he even try to contact me? What kind of father does that?"

They met at a Sizzler, and I drove that day to be a supportive friend. Dan wanted a public place as he was uncertain as to how the encounter would unfold. In a private one, the meeting might get heated and out of hand. And Dan wanted to confront him with the absent father pain he felt throughout his life. When they met face-to-face he boldly said, "I need to tell you that for all my life, I've been angry at you. All my life, I've been hurt by you. All my life I've been frustrated by the fact everybody else could talk about their dad and I didn't even know who my dad was." He wanted to say all these things and then forgive him.

It's quite a sight to see a friend go in to a meeting all wound up and leave with a sense of release and a true peace. It's a powerful moment; we knew God was right there with us. When forgiveness needs to be great and great forgiveness occurs, it's amazing; you've seen God work.

There's a movie entitled *Heaven's Rain*. It portrays the story of Brooks Douglass. He was the son of Southern Baptist missionary parents in Brazil, who returned to Oklahoma, where his father became pastor of Putnam City Baptist Church. One night, October 13, 1979, sixteen-year-old Brooks Douglass let two drifters into their home. They robbed the family, raped his twelve-year-old sister and shot all four bound family members before leaving them for dead. Richard and Marilyn Douglass died at the scene. Bleeding and faint, Leslie managed to help untie Brooks who, despite his own wounds, got her to the family car and drove them both to a doctor, who in turn got them to a hospital in time to save their lives.

The movie goes on to show how God, throughout the years, not overnight, not even easily, brought them to the point of forgiveness. The movie ends with an eight-minute scene summarizing Douglass's ninety-minute prison meeting in 1995 with murderer Glenn Ake during which Douglass let go of hate and anger bottled up for years and forgave the triggerman who changed his life.

Recycling takes you through the forgiveness process as many times as need be, perhaps for the rest of your life, so that you can and do, release what's owed you to the Lord, for His collection.

The predominant reason we recycle is because we need time, time for the pain to fade, powerful memories to dim, and our scars to heal. Our emotions need time to recover.

Time doesn't do it all; you understand. The notion that time heals all wounds, while partially true, is far from absolute. Forgiveness is what heals, but often, forgiveness takes time.

Another truth to consider: secrecy doesn't help us. Secrets keep us sick. Forgiveness is delayed or lost altogether when you keep the fact of your forgiveness to yourself. There is healing in revealing you've forgiven. "I want you to know, I have forgiven you, I have turned it over to the Lord." It's healthy, and it puts an end to it.

But what if the person you're forgiving is dead? My now dead grandfather sexually abused my sisters, and I didn't find out about it until a long time after he was dead. The good news is I didn't have to kill him myself. I'm not saying I would have, but I sure thought about it. I had to forgive him. This meant I had to consider my own sin and how God had forgiven me. I even had to think about some of my big offenses He'd covered with Jesus blood. I, then, needed to articulate to another person my feelings and how I wanted to forgive him. Next, I actually wrote him a letter. I detailed what I'd found out, what I felt about it, and that I was choosing to forgive him. Does that mean I never think about it anymore, or that it just goes away, along with the pain? No, it doesn't mean that. But it does mean healing can't start until you acknowledge the violation. And healing won't go very far if you hold your hurts secretly inside

Acknowledge the offense to God, bring another person into the process, and ultimately, confront the offender. Had I been able to confront my grandfather as Dan confronted his long absent father? Would I have seen him repent? I doubt it. Dan didn't see his father repent either. After Dan told his father that his father's absence had caused him fifty-four years of pain and hardship, his father said very little, and he never apologized and never said how sorry he was. He certainly didn't ask for forgiveness. But Noel's drunk driver did. He was repentant. He felt horrible about what he'd done, and how he'd cost Noel and his family so very much. However, him feeling horrible didn't heal Noel, or take the pain away, and Dan's father's indifference didn't prevent Dan from healing and neither did my having to resort to a letter to the dead. Forgiveness heals and how the object of your forgiveness reacts to it, matters not. In fact, healing comes when we honor God by being grace givers to those who've wounded us.

Two Parts of Forgiveness

Mercy

There are two parts to forgiveness. One is mercy—God's mercy to us, the foundation of his forgiveness of us and our relationship with Him. Mercy is an act of rescue, snatching us from what we deserve. In our case, the fires of hell, and placing us where we could only aspire to—in our case, into His family, then heaven. We, because we have been given mercy, now give mercy, but not back to God, because He doesn't need it, but to the people who harm us. They deserve our wrath and retribution, but instead, we extend them mercy by not punishing them. And God approves. "Blessed are the merciful, for they will be shown mercy" (Matt. 5:7). But we're not to stop there. Matthew 5:44–45 says, "But I tell you, love your enemies and pray for those who persecute you, that you may be children of your Father in heaven." But mercy to those who've wronged us goes even beyond this. Romans 12:20 admonishes us this way, "On the contrary: 'If your enemy is hungry, feed him; if he is thirsty, give him something to drink. In doing this, you will heap burning coals on his head.'" We are commanded to be proactive in our mercy just as God was proactive in His mercy to us. He didn't just rescue us from the pits of hell then leave us far better off on the side of the road. But He provides abundantly for us for life and beyond, adopts us into his family, making us coheirs with His only begotten son. Above all that, gives us the unfathomable privilege of knowing Him, seeing Him, and having Him work through us. Of course, the object of our mercy might still have civil penalties to pay. Noel's did, and had my grandfather lived, he would have to, believe me. That's governmental forgiveness as you recall. But in such cases, mercy may extend to visiting our enemy in their punishment.

Grace

Which bring up forgiveness's second part—grace. Sometimes, it's hard to tell when mercy ends and grace begins. Grace is unmerited favor. Where mercy is rescue from the negative, grace is replacing deserved negative with positive—unmerited favor. After you've knifed me in the back, I choose to treat you better than you deserve, not for a time, but for always.

We need to make something clear. Forgiveness, mercy, and grace do not necessarily add up to reconciliation. If someone's *done you wrong*, betrayed you, harmed you, threatened you, done anything to you that breaks your trust, makes being anywhere near them unsafe, then don't trust them and don't put yourself in danger again. Do only what makes sense or what you know God is leading you to do. And if danger is involved, don't go alone and without counsel beforehand. The enemy is out there and he'd love to do you harm as well. Predators are clever, that's how they've remained alive. Satan is the chief predator. He is a liar. And one of their most deadly codependent traps is this lie—unless you restore the relationship to the way it was, you haven't forgiven. Not true. Forgiveness is letting go of your right to retribution and, if it makes sense, working to plant and water seeds that God may later bring to harvest. Restoration, if it's in God's plan at all, may take years to relationship reconstruct.

Understanding and putting forgiveness into practice requires you understand where to draw a line in the sand; the one between you having forgiven and you giving trust or respect in blind human faith. After forgiveness, there's no requirement for vulnerability, except with Jesus. He's your avenger now. And remember, keep those hands in your pocket; don't grab back what you have given away.

Remember, you can talk to people you don't trust or respect. And you can be kind to them. You don't talk evil about them or say they're bad people. They, like you and I, are sinners saved by grace. They, like you and I, have fallen short of God's glory. They, like you and I, still sin, only our hate of it, and God's work within us drives us to our knees. In fact, the proof of their salvation was the Holy Spirit's work to bring them to repentance. But trust? Not yet. They are not honored with being our confidant or given knowledge of our vulnerabilities. But we do choose to treat them with the personal dignity of being made in His image and worthy of respect in that light.

Our battle cry to forgive is the ongoing discipline of permitting ourselves to be found in His love daily. To abide in Him, receiving forgiveness in our own life, and wanting Him more than any outcomes from people and circumstances. Maintaining an insatiable thirst to know God not just for His gifts but first and foremost, for His heart and character is the starting point at which forgiveness can birth in any lasting relationship.

SERVING AND BLESSING

We now turn our attention to being a servant and a blessing in our relationships. Two related but separate concepts, but two very important ones when you want a relationship to last. Look at those relationships you have that are lasting and warm—friendships you've had for a long time. In all probability, these folks have compassionate hearts that serve and bless you.

So what's the difference between serving and blessing? We all know what an act of service is. Something someone does for us. Our neighbor washes our car. A friend invites us to a game we want to see, or stops at the drug store for us when we're under the weather. Someone serves us. But what is a blessing? It's more than serving us what we need; it's going above and beyond—we get what we need, what we want, what we may enjoy. Let me give you an example.

My daughter blessed my wife last night. When we got back into town yesterday evening, my wife didn't feel well at all. As soon as my daughter heard about it, she went to Albertson's and bought everything needed to make her favorite—chicken noodle soup—then made it from scratch. To the basic broth, she adds and simmers all the things my wife loves and then brings it over. My daughter went out of her way to be a blessing to her mom. Don't you just want to be around those people? It's just comforting to spend time with them. Life just goes better when they're nearby.

What kind of people do you not want to be around? Folks who know you're struggling know you have basic needs being unmet and hardly even acknowledge the fact; they leave any help you might need to someone else. "Stop whining. God helps those who help themselves." If you want relationships to last, you have to be a servant, and you also need to take it to the next level. You need to be a blessing; you need to go above and beyond.

My daughter could have bought Campbell's Chicken Noodle soup and just heated it up. She could've gone to Trader Joe's and bought the premade, quart size soup. That would have been good enough. But she didn't. She took the time to go the market, buy exactly what her mother likes, and made it on her own stove, in her own cookware, and then delivered it with a nice note and some flowers. Although my wife didn't feel well, it was a long time before the smile left her lips and that warm spot in her heart cooled off. In fact, it hasn't cooled off yet. That's being a blessing to someone. And in relationships, it matters. Of course, you don't have the time to raise every relationship you have to that level. But relationships you want to focus on, for instance, are with your parents, siblings, key people at work, and at school, important college professors—particularly those who teach you about relationships. Those relationships that matter most and those you want to nurture, those surrounded by love and caring, all need to be moved up to the next level—the "be a blessing" level.

How about those special relationships, the boyfriend/girlfriend relationship? What if you're blessing the socks off your friend, but you are being ignored? Let's say he gets sick as my wife did, and you, knowing what he likes, head over to the store and put together a care package for him. He loves it, says all the right things, let's you know you really hit the spot. A week later, you've caught what he had. And he refuses even to come over. "You don't want me to catch it again, do you? When you're better, give me a call."

What's that tell you? He doesn't care. Or at least, he doesn't care like you care. I suppose he could say, "I didn't know you wanted a care package? How would I know that? And how would

I know what to put in it? But all people like a care package when they're sick. Who cares what's in it.

And since we're talking about caring, it's obvious he doesn't care like you care. Where are you on his priority list? A care package would have taken a little time, money, imagination, and energy. What did he spend those on while you were ill? A movie? Pizza with the guys after a scrimmage basketball game? You know he loves basketball. And that game would have taken a lot more time and energy, maybe even imagination, than a box with some treats in it. Just one candy treat, that's all it would have taken. You love Snickers. He didn't go above and beyond; he tunneled below and nowhere near. It's one thing to say, "I'm really sorry you don't feel well. I'm praying for you." Which, by the way, is a good thing. But to take time and write a card, or pick up *her* favorite flowers or others of *his* favorite things, that's an amazing act of caring; that's bestowing a blessing. And in doing so, it's a strong step in relationship building characterized by sweetness and kindness.

If guys or gals don't initiate or reciprocate these blessings, these thoughtful acts of generosity and kindness when you're dating, why would you think they'd initiate or reciprocate if you married them? Please understand me, these blessings you bestow aren't given so that you get back later. We're not trying to "guilt" someone into caring for us or act kindly toward us. Bestowing a blessing is a selfless act of caring, perhaps of love. If it never comes back, that's okay. But it does reveal a caring, selfless heart, like the heart we want to marry. I think if a relationship is to be effective and lasting, both spouses must have selfless, caring hearts. Initiating and reciprocating reveals this heart, reveals the spouses are at least conscious of the needs and wants of their mates and are willing to expend their personal resources—time, energy, money, imagination—to do their best to fulfill them. Even when they might not get the warm smile in return they hope for. Bestowing a blessing is about giving without expectation of return. And it's also about going that extra mile for someone who's gone that extra mile for us.

The scriptural principal for this is 1 John 3:16. Not John 3:16 (as pivotal as that verse is), but 1 John 3:16. "By this we know love; that he laid down his life for us, and we ought to lay down our lives for the brothers" (ESV). Remember, while we were yet sinners, yet enemies of God, working with our whole hearts to defeat Him, He died for us, took our punishment on the cross, so that we might become God's children. Now I don't think this verse is telling us to go around dying for people. After all, we would only be able to do that once. Of course, if that sacrifice needs to be made, God will make it clear to us. I do believe, though, he's telling us to die to ourselves, put ourselves in the backseat when it comes to our relationship with other believers, and particularly, those close to us. Even though the situation may not call for us to dive in front of a bus for someone, but our desire to be a blessing may be calling us to take a few minutes to pick up a card and write a note to someone who needs a bit of cheer or encouragement. "I hope you're feeling better" or "Sorry you're going through a difficult time." If you're not willing to spend a few minutes this way, when called to make a real sacrifice, you'll certainly balk. And that's what's being pictured here—sacrifice— true sacrifice, 1 John 3:16 sacrifice.

Elisabeth Elliot is a remarkable woman. She and her first husband, Jim Elliott, were missionaries to Ecuador in the fifties. In 1956, while attempting to make contact with the Auca natives of eastern Ecuador, he and several others were killed. One of her books *Through Gates of Splendor* describes the incident and how she and her daughter returned to the Auca to evangelize them and ultimately lead the one who killed her husband to the Lord. Not long ago, the movie *End of the Spear* told this story as well. She is now a respected author of at least twenty books and sought-after speaker. A common theme through all her books as you can imagine is service to others. And when expanding upon 1 John 3:16, she actually expressed the notion found there into a few, very powerful words. This verse, to her, simply but profoundly means *my life for yours.*

Who doesn't want to have a relationship with those who are willing to sacrifice something from their life so that they might give the other something they need or want? And to have a lasting relationship with someone like that is straight from heaven. And when I say life, I'm talking about giving of your time, talents, imagination, and your resources. If a person isn't willing to do that, then what kind of relationship is it? Think about it. What kind of relationship is that? If they're not willing to give up anything in their life for you, if they take but seldom or never give, how would you characterize or describe that kind of relationship?

It's definitely lopsided. The scales tip radically to one side assuming, of course, that you're bestowing blessings. That kind of relationship is self-centered and perhaps even egocentric. The world revolves around the other person. They take and take because they believe they deserve to take and take. They may whisper sweet nothings in your ear. They may also be gifted, charming, have time up the wahzoo, be geniuses, and incredibly inventive. They may even be rich. But if they're not willing to sacrifice some of what they possess for you, your relationship with them is, at best, one-sided. Ideally, what makes a lasting relationship is when both give without concern for getting when both bless the other without concern for whether the other is reciprocating. Love keeps no record of right or wrong; it just is. When both are giving and both live sacrificially, both feel cared for, wanted, and blessed. But if one becomes, or both become self-centered and egocentric, then the connection between the two quickly strains. Neither feels loved, wanted, or blessed.

This self-centeredness can be an issue of maturity—boys becoming men, girls becoming women, which we will discuss in detail in subsequent chapters. When we're kids, it's all about us. That attitude is natural in the developmental stages of life. Being a baby, infant, child, even a youth—tween or teen—it's all about them being served by others. A baby or infant cries when it's hungry and is fed. A child sneaks a candy bar bought by its parents. A tweener or teener comes home from school and when left

89

alone in the kitchen for two minutes, eats whatever's in the fridge put there by mom, even if mom planned to have it for dinner. It's all about them. They do nothing to provide for themselves and that's as it should be. But it's supposed to change when they graduate high school, certainly by the time they graduate college. It is no longer about self. It's about those he or she loves; it about moving closer and closer to the image of Christ; Christ who died for us. We're not supposed to be a takers but servants.

Of course, some may say, "But I get a lot of joy from making her happy" or "But it's so much fun just to be around him. I consider all the giving I do as the price I have to pay." Well, holding a baby is fun, and a baby doesn't give you anything either. There is a great deal of joy in holding your child even though the little guy might spit up all over you. But the reality is, the joy is intrinsic to the relationship between parent and child. Most people aren't willing to give up their sleep, energy, and clothing for someone else's kid. Unless paid to do it. One-sided relationships, no matter how much "fun" they are in the beginning, no matter how much joy giving brings, eventually grow strained.

When one of the pair hordes—time, energy, imagination, resources—when he or she lives by the adage "What's mine is mine and what's yours is mine too," the relationship is in trouble, maybe not immediately but soon. I think we've all been exposed to relationships like that. How do you feel after a while? Do you feel endeared to that person? Do you feel like you can hardly wait to spend the rest of your life with this person? No. You feel you're being used, taken for granted, not appreciated, and when they actually ask you to do something for them, angry. Why? Because as hard as we do to be the Christ-like servants, there's a part of us who wants to be blessed as well. When we go above and beyond, we want to see a little reciprocation. We want to see at least a little coming back. Not necessarily because we want to get stuff; we just want to know the other person cares about us enough to considers our feelings and want us to be happy, cares about what we want, what we need, and is willing to put him, or herself out for us.

We don't serve and bless others in order to get something back. Please understand that. It's never a positive for us before God to want to imitate the servant heart just to get things back. No. Remember, it's my life for yours. Focus on others. If, however, the person you're spending your time with, whether a family member, roommate, teammate, or a boyfriend or girlfriend, when it becomes one-sided or lopsided and you're initiating activities to serve without reciprocation, blessings without reciprocation, the relationship will become lifeless and cold. In fact, there's a name for it in the game of chess. We call it a *stalemate*, and aptly, nobody wins.

As the opponents stare at their pieces and board position, they know it's over. There's no movement, no growth. The two of you are stuck. Sound familiar to anyone? I know it does to some of you who have already been in relationships where you feel stuck—no way up, no way down, no way out. And the reason boils down to this: you are blessing your socks off and getting zip back. It's like looking into dead eyes. But maybe it's not you. Maybe it's a friend or loved one; maybe you see the one-sidedness of their relationship and your heart goes out to him or her. What are your thoughts about all this?

If you've ever been on the initiating-servant end of a relationship, initiating blessing after blessing and your mate just won't, can't, or is too clueless to know he or she should reciprocate, sometimes you try to step things up. We think, *If I can just do a little more, be even more thoughtful, even more imaginative, expend just a little more effort, even become more intuitive so I can anticipate what he'll need, then he'll get the picture, then he'll love me enough to care enough.* Usually he won't. Getting what he deserves is the focus of his life. In the quiet of his room, when he's summarizing all that matters to him, he mutters, "I'm number one. Therefore, it's only natural that I'm loved, that those who love me most do things for me—serve and bless me. That's what they're here for. Serving me has to be the high point of their day."

At the beginning of a relationship, the balance may be a bit one-sided. When two different people, perhaps from different backgrounds, with different goals for a relationship, come together, it's natural that one may bless the other more often, with more thought and effort. It could be that blessing—going above and beyond—is just in that person's DNA. Blessings may be a natural part of their family life, or that might be a thousand other influences on this issue. However, as relationships develop and grow between two healthy individuals, reciprocal giving increases. Be aware, though, sometimes you may be more into the relationship than the other and a lack of reciprocation is the other's little way of telling you this. "I just want to hang out. I'm not into anything serious right now or anything I have to think too much about. I have a degree to get. When I get that, then things might be different. Right now, don't make me work too hard. Let's just have fun." Either way, the lack of reciprocation will kill the relationship quickly.

You bring up the question, "How come when it comes to your needs, even your wants, I bend over backward to provide them to you as best I can. But when it comes to my needs, you don't respond the same way? It's like you don't even care." The other gets indignant. "What are you talking about? Just last night when you had to go home from the library early, didn't I tell you it was okay and let you walk home alone when you wanted? Why do you even question that I care for you. Don't I tell you? When you made all my favorite things for dinner the other evening, didn't I thank you before I left for the roller derby? You know you'd like the roller derby if you'd give it another try. The skaters very seldom land on the audience. I'm sure that lightning wouldn't strike you twice that way."

I was in an airport one day when I overheard a conversation that gives us a full-color picture of just what we're talking about, illustrating how the world ignores the spiritual to their own emotional peril. Now, I don't work at eavesdropping; it just comes naturally when people are nearby and they're talking more loudly than they ought. This young lady was doing just that, probably because she was getting just a bit heated.

From the sounds of it, they weren't married but were cohabitating. I got that from her overriding, theme-setting question of him. "When are you ever gonna deliver on the promise of a ring?" And since I was sitting behind them for three hours, I heard that question in various forms several times.

She was just pretty worked up about the situation she was beginning to understand she was hip deep in. It seems they were flying back from his parent's house and she pushed this right in his face: "Okay, what year are we going to spend the holiday with my family? Huh? Ten years from now? Fifteen? For the last five years—in a row, I might add—we fly three thousand miles—"

"Two thousand five hundred," he corrected.

"Twenty-five hundred's a lot better. I'm much calmer now." Actually, she was getting more heated, "Okay, Two thousand five hundred to see your family—that uncle of yours with the two teeth. When are we going to spend a holiday with my family? When?"

"I—"

"And when am I going to get the ring? When!"

As if getting the ring, being engaged, getting married was going to change anything, or going to change him. She imagines in ten years when they've been married five, she'd be able to look back and say, "It all changed when you gave me that ring. You used to be a selfish, egotistical, uncaring, manipulator, but when you slipped that cubic zirconium on my finger, that one I thought was a diamond for so long, you became all the man I really wanted—sweet, cherishing, and willing to do anything to make me happy."

But facts are facts. If your boy or girlfriend isn't willing to sacrifice for you when you're dating, when that spark of love is still warm and bright, what makes you think he'll make those cherishing sacrifices after the deals sealed? The conversation was hard to listen to but we managed, and the gist of it was everything we've just talked about. She was saying in no uncertain terms, "I'm the one giving, giving, giving. You're the one taking, taking, taking. It's not going to go on like this forever." And now she was upping the ante, ratcheting her requests—her demands—to a higher priority. He was either going to take her seriously, or it was going to be over. The scary thing is, to keep the status quo, he might just make more promises, maybe even give her the ring and set the date. Maybe begin to give her just enough to keep her quiet. He continues to siphon off the top of their relationship, continuing to take this poor girl for all she's got, while only investing dribs and drabs of his own. Ladies, gentlemen, look at the heart as best you are able. Don't fool or lie to yourself. Face the reality of what God's showing you. Without the firm, loving, morphing hand of Christ, the selfish remain selfish. The relationships grounded in the world are all that way.

Since, though, you want one grounded in heaven, what is the telltale sign that you've got one? Relationships go in cycles, and generally, in springtime and summer, when the weather's nice, things are little more laid-back, life moves at a more accommodating pace, and we're more willing to be accommodating in our relationships. There's a greater propensity to just do what the other person wants to do. So when a relationship starts up, say over summer, both are more willing to accommodate the other. What do you want to do? Well, I want to go eat wherever you want to eat. You want to see a movie? What movie? I want to see whatever movie you want to go see. Dating is accommo*dating* in the beginning stages.

If you've been in a relationship for months or years and you're still having to accommodate the other, the relationship is lopsided. Marrying or having children with that person won't change it. I wish it would, but the principal of non-determination applies. We cannot change people. We don't have the power. But God does. When we want a person to change, we pray, present our requests to the Lord, and if God agrees, He'll work and the people will change. Admittedly, some change is simply growing up and realizing all isn't about you anymore. And for men, that may take a while. Men just do not mature as fast as women do. Case in point, my cousin Emily is twenty-seven, and she is marrying a guy who's thirty-six. Big age difference, huh?

But often, men take some extra years to get down that maturity road and discover that life isn't just about them. Of course, you can be a woman and very self-centered too at any age. But generally speaking, at the age you are now, men are trailing a little behind. Check out a seventh grade class. The girls are prom-ready, the boys are Scooby-Doo ready.

Generally, men in the culture of North America don't mature physically or emotionally as fast as women do. There are exceptions; it's not an absolute truism. Look at the physical and some emotional characteristics of adolescent girls compared to guys, or ask a classroom teacher of these age groups to confirm this assertion. So decide. Do you want a mature, reciprocating relationship where you might be of different ages? Or do you want to wait until the man of your dreams grows up? Either way, if maturity and each providing initiated and reciprocated blessings to the other is a goal, which I hope by now it is, you'll also be opting for a relationship that has a good opportunity to be a long lasting relationship. Did you catch that, initiating and reciprocating blessings? If you just reciprocate, that's not a bad thing but the more mature action is to initiate blessings as well.

Just to put a point on it. Reciprocating a blessing is when your mate bestows a blessing on you. You, in response, bestowed one back; one at least as thoughtful and sacrificial. Initiating is what your mate did to you in the first place. He or she bestowed a blessing on you first. Frankly, it's important that you see blessings initiated early in the relationship soon after the just getting-to-know-you phase. Because that's when you guys are most focused on one another. If it doesn't happen then, it probably won't happen at all.

I saw this early in my relationship with Roxanna. Every chance she had she offered to help—type papers, filing, anything. This is back when dinosaurs roamed the earth and they communicated via typewriters. She typed very fast, so I'd write everything long hand, and she would type whatever I needed. A couple times a week, she'd call and ask if I had anything to type. If I didn't, I'd write up something real quick so I could see her. That servant heart of hers was there from the very beginning when we were students together. We met in grad school and dated for about a year. Then we broke up for two years because of me. I graduated and was a year ahead of her. I robbed the cradle but then left the relationship for a job. But actually, I wasn't ready to commit as yet; something I still had to deal with later. But even in the very first months of our relationship, she would take her time, energy, and other resources and bestow blessings upon me. I remember being sick, got food poisoning at a retreat I spoke at. I ate some food that had been sitting around a while in the lake cabin—longer than I realized—and it messed me up bad.

I spent a couple days in the hospital, and when I was released and finally got home, I was still pretty weak. We'd only been dating three or four months, but every day, faithfully, she brought me a care package. A movie she rented for me to enjoy. I'd lost quite a bit of weight, so she brought my favorite snacks such as Whoppers for lunch—thoughtful things like that. Her heart for blessings was active from the very beginning. And it's no different today. That's who she was then; that's who she is today. If blessing comes from a mature place, initiation and reciprocation won't go away. I've never heard of that happening. Either the heart is there to serve and to bless—not just yourself—or it's not. Roxanna and I have been married twenty-nine years, and I've known her for thirty-two. She's the same loving, giving person now as she was then. And because of her, I've tried to step up. I've not always succeeded, but over the years, I've tried to do a lot of neat things for her too. And I still do. Just as she brought me those care packages so many years ago, when we're having a difficult day, we surprise each other with goodies. While my daughter cooked chicken soup for her last night, I went to the store and got some of her favorite things too. When she woke up today, I had a cozy fire going in the fireplace and a pile of Christmasy, snacky foods so all day she could be cozy warm and surrounded by familiar comforts. Why? Because she does that for me in abundance.

Right now, I feel like I'm the reciprocator. She initiates quite often, and I try to reciprocate just as often. I feel like I need to do better. Blessing one another makes for a lasting relationship. And if it's not there in the beginning, don't think it will show up later. Again, people can mature; they can grow up. And they may grow to a selfless, giving place, but you can't count on it. Don't commit yourself to someone long term that hasn't achieved a level of maturity where they are no longer egocentric; life is not just about them. Another telltale sign: egocentricity shows up in other places too. Self-centered and egocentric people just don't want to help other people. It's not just you. If a roommate needs something, the roommate's on his own. If their family needs help, they're on their own as well. If you see that trait, run. Conversely, if people are selfless to their mates, they take time for other people as well. Meaning, they're willing to volunteer, maybe to tutor kids after school, or help out older folk. Perhaps they give up their time to go on mission trips to Mexico to build homes for the homeless, or churches for God's people. They sacrifice to serve other people. Maybe you don't see the person sacrificing so much for you yet, but see the person serving others in other relationships. You know the person is willing and capable of spending their time and talents on others. Maybe you time will come as your relationship matures.

Another indicator: where people spend their money. When people only spend money on themselves, they're spending it on the most important person in their lives—themselves. They become living proof of the spiritual principal God reveals in Matthew 6:2, "For where your treasure is, there your heart will be also" (NIV). When that treasure is for your use only, your heart is too.

God doesn't want that. He wants our hearts focused on others and on the good works He's prepared for us to do. Our treasure needs to be in Him. Often selfish people are frightened people. They spend all their treasure on themselves because they ultimately believe they are the only ones who will. They're fundamentally alone in the universe. They have to keep all they have and accumulate more, or they might just run out one day. God tells us just the opposite. In Matthew 6:25–30 (NIV) as our Lord Jesus speaks His sermon from the mount, he says:

> Therefore I tell you, do not be anxious about your life, what you will eat or what you will drink, nor about your body, what you will put on. Is not life more than food, and the body more than clothing? Look at the birds of the air: they neither sow nor reap nor gather into barns, and yet your heavenly Father feeds them. Are you not of more value than they? And which of you by being anxious can add a single hour to his span of life? And why are you anxious about clothing? Consider the lilies of the field, how they grow: they neither toil nor spin, yet I tell you, even Solomon in all his glory was not arrayed like one of these. But if God so clothes the grass of the field, which today is alive and tomorrow is thrown into the oven, will he not much more clothe you, O you of little faith?

Think we should spend any time at all worrying? No, not a nanosecond.

So free your heart from worry, and give. Your daddy owns the cattle on a thousand hills, and He's promised to care for you better than you can possibly care for yourself. Where your treasures are, that's where your heart really is.

Who you spend your time with, share your talents, and your money on is who you really love. So, if you can't give to other people, you really love yourself. And self-love will not fashion a lasting relationship. Servant-centered love will; the principle of my life for yours will. Why would anyone want to be in a relationship with someone who doesn't exhibit that principle? Yet many are in such relationships. Why?

One reason might be that self-centered, self-serving people can be charming, intelligent, and quite successful. They may have good jobs and a lot of money. Maybe you see such a person and you find him or her attractive, even captivating and you figure that's a good thing even though you have to be the one who gives. At least you'll get some pretty sizeable crumbs that fall from his or her table. "This may be the best I'm going to do." Self-centered and self-serving people always want relationships with people who are willing to give them all they have. Like I said, everybody wants to be in a relationship that gives them everything. But even for all the crumbs the givers pick up, people want to be loved, and being fed the dregs shows them they are not. What other reasons people might stay in a lopsided relationship? Besides a fear that nothing better will come along.

They may idealize the relationship. They may lie to themselves; tell themselves their mates really do love them. Perhaps they even ascribe the label of "blessing" to some pretty meager services. "But he does help me around the house. When was that? A month ago? When he set the table. Well, not all of it, but he got me the forks. That's a blessing, right?" And they might take this stance because they simply believe they don't deserve any better. For whatever reason, they're willing to take less because they believe they are less. When you have that diminutive view of yourself, and minimize yourself, you will tolerate a lot, even tolerate an egocentric relationship.

A danger in this type of thinking is that you begin to believe what value you do have comes from this relationship. "He's handsome, charming, and rich, and he's decided to be with me. I must be valuable because of that." Our value comes from God; we have no value outside of Christ. Yet when we come into the kingdom, when we take Jesus Christ as our personal Lord and Savior, we become children of the king, heirs with Christ.

Why else would people put up with a lopsided relationship? People may feel the role of giver is one they can play, one they'll achieve some security playing. As long as you keep giving, giving, giving, the person receiving will be happy in the relationship. And that's the most important thing, that person who is happy is satisfied with you. However, a time will come when you want a relationship that's more "balanced," more of a two-way relationship, where you are loved as much as you love, where you receive as much as you give because your mate loves you enough to give in return.

A student shared that her roommate had a boyfriend, an athlete who is going to the Olympics in Spain. He's a very immature, self-centered person, and the relationship is a very lopsided, but she remains with him because she likes having a prominent athlete as her boyfriend! We place people on pedestals and decide a relationship with them is worth whatever it takes. A person's motivation can be many things besides the desire for a healthy relationship. Maybe I want a secure financial future so I marry a surgeon who's an egomaniac. You'll always have a good income. "Even though it's lopsided, I'm secure. I'll always have money." Being financially secure is something we aspire to, but to trade your emotional happiness for it, denies the fact that God has promised to provide. Your financial security is in Him, just as our eternal security is. What other things keep people in relationships like that? I can think of at least one more thing. The fear of losing what they have. So the myth is created that says if they give enough, serve long enough, do whatever they can as often as they can to make their mates happy, one day their mates will wake up and realize how valuable they are and love them back.

There's another reason to consider. If you've given yourself sexually to somebody, a bond forms. And that bond may keep you in a stuck and unhealthy relationship for a long time. I personally have observed this truth. Sexual intimacy is a bond that forms, and it's strong. That's why you need to be careful. That's why scripture encourages us to wait for marriage. Don't give yourself away sexually to anyone before the marriage ceremony. And before you marry someone, make sure they're mature, selfless, and one of God's children. Otherwise, the bond that's formed emotionally may be with someone who cannot function in a healthy relationship with you. And you feel stuck; you're committed because of an intangible bond that formed from just plain lust. Then ten to twenty years down the road, they're married, have children, and they hate their life. Or at least one person hates his or her life. The other one just keeps taking and taking.

When asked to describe their relationship, their stories are remarkably similar. They became sexually active in college, then she got pregnant, and they decided they should get married. The self-centered partner has never changed. But the bond of sexual intimacy was formed and then another bond formed—marriage. Did marriage fix anything? Did marriage make a healthy relationship from the one they had? Not really; it just made the trap more inescapable. The physical, emotional bond has become a legal commitment; the end of which is alimony and child support and worse, broken hearts and broken lives. The unhealthy relationship continued and morphed into a destructive force.

If a guy or a gal—and it can go both ways—pressures you to give yourself sexually to them, you're the one who's doing the giving and the other the receiving. The one pressuring is the one getting. It's not for you at all.

Do you see how lopsided that is? And I know people under that pressure. I've talked to many of them. "I keep telling him where my boundaries are, and he keeps pushing me to cross them. Why?" It's for him. And that's another indicator of a lopsided relationship. If people are not willing to delay gratification until the long-term commitment at the altar, then they're thinking of only themselves. In fact, this may be the earliest sign of a self-centered mate, and a lopsided relationship. Your mate wants to gratify him or herself sexually at your expense. At the expense of your values, your convictions, your relationship with the God of the universe. Which, of course, brings into question the pressurer's relationship with Him. No matter how you look at this situation, it's not about serving you.

Stay together for the sake of the children. This may be a noble reason. We all know the devastating impact divorce has on children. Another reason? Sometimes, people are desperate to escape a bad family situation—physical and/or sexual abuse, or uncaring parents. If they can find someone who's not going to abuse them, or strong enough to protect them, for them, it's a good trade. "At least I'm safe." This lopsided relationship may not be perfect, but it's a lot better than the one they were in. Don't settle for less in your life and relationships. God's plan is for you to receive from others and to be blessed as you give.

There are many reasons one can come up with to remain in an unhealthy, lopsided relationship, make sure you're not coming up with one. And if you think you might be, go to the Lord with your concerns. He's there to help you now and redeem your past relationship patterns and choices.

BOYS TO MEN

In have observed and noted a consistent theme when couples are having relationship problems. I hear wives regularly comment about their husbands immaturity, "You know, I feel like I'm raising three boys, one seven, one nine, and one in his thirties!" She married a guy who's supposed to be grown up, mature enough to be a responsible man at home and be present. And he's not. Of course, she's be much ahead if she'd recognized his immaturity at the beginning of a relationship. But as we've mentioned before, when a relationship begins, one's always accommodating the other. A guy may act grown-up for a while. Even I can manage it for a few weeks at a time. Women can as well. In the next chapter, Roxanna will discuss what it means for girls to grow up and become women. But now we're talking about men and how they mature and ways to recognize levels of maturity.

Now, let me make it clear. People can grow. They can change. Maturity can develop at any stage or age in life. If you are a mature woman, you don't want to be in a relationship where a few minutes of your day involves raising an adult to adulthood, do you? Immaturity is not necessarily a character flaw; however, there may be an issue if a thirty- or forty-year-old continues to engage in the kind of mischief—sin—a teen or younger might. Developmental experts tell us men don't mature as quickly as women do physiologically, emotionally, and intellectually. In a classroom with preteens, you can see it. Take a look sometime at

103

fifth and sixth graders. The girls look ready for a prom; the guys are giggling and shooting spit wads.

But men eventually catch up physically, but more importantly, emotionally. And that's a very good thing. Paul confirms it here. "When I was a child, I spoke like a child, I thought like a child, I reasoned like a child. When I became a man, I gave up childish ways" (1 Cor. 13:11). Paul recognized there's a time to be a child and do as a child does. Even though kids often grow up too quickly in our culture, it's okay for a kid to be a kid, but when it comes time to take on the responsibilities of a serious relationship, you've got to put childish things away.

We're going to explore what that means as we look at some of the characteristics of a mature guy. But first of all, just for fun, let's look at some ways you can recognize a spiritual boy—not a spiritual man or a spiritual person—but a *spiritual boy*. For a few pages, let's pretend we're on *Letterman*, and we've got a list of twelve ways to spot an immature, spiritual boy.

1. Although married, he will not drive a minivan and insists on buying a sleek two-seater sports car. Then weeks from getting married, he decides he can't afford the perfect apartment for him and his soon-to-be bride because of his sports car payment. Is a relationship more important than the car?

2. When a man has more toys than his children do—golf clubs, X-boxes, pool table, video games, ATVs, wave runners, Jet Skis, dune buggies—but his kids can't go to Christian school because he can't afford it

3. He may work and earn income. If he wants something, he buys it, whether he can afford it or not. His retirement plan is to die young. And he's his favorite person to buy presents for. He sees credit cards as his savings account; they keep delayed gratification at bay. How a person manages finances says something about their maturity level.

4. A job generally interferes with his free time and a job held more than six months is considered a career.
5. Chores around the house are defined by what he won't do. "I won't do laundry. I won't do toilets. Second-storey story windows are her problem (heights give me nose bleeds as does any kind of work), and I don't empty a dishwasher; it just fills up again." Being a helpmate is a selective thing. Just do what needs to be done? You're kidding, right?
6. A sub-clause in the prenup he insists on starts with, "Party of the first part, when asked by the party of the second part to change the party of the third part's diaper, may ignore said question, and the first ten times asked may guffaw loudly and say, "Yeah, right!" I suggest you tear up the prenup and don't marry the guy. How can a relationship survive with that level of maturity?
7. Laying down your life for your wife means you spend the football season prone on the couch.
8. The guy spent $10,965 on Lakers season tickets and gives twenty bucks a week at church, when he goes. His idea of giving to a Christian ministry is bringing a neighbor's two sticks of butter to the youth groups baked potato night. If a guy doesn't have time or money to serve in a church but has both for his own entertainment, maturity for him is still an elusive goal. If he continues as he is, he will never make a godly father for your children.
9. He refuses to be submissive to anybody. He can never work for anyone because he can't submit to anybody. He won't follow anyone because he has to be in charge. "If I ain't in charge, I ain't workin'." Maturity recognizes that God has ordained authority, and there are some things we just have to do and be able to do. Especially when it comes to following the laws of the land, and the rules of the condo. Not following one of the rules cost me $250 this morning. And it wasn't even my fault! We're allowed two stickers for our

two cars and a guest pass for a guest's cars. The guest pass is to be displayed on the dashboard, or you run the risk of being towed. My son forgot to display his guest pass on the car he borrowed from me. I kept telling him and telling him, and yesterday, the hammer fell. And this morning, I paid $250 to get my car out of impound because my son just didn't want to submit to a rule. Now it's time for him to grow up and take responsibility, about $250 worth. Ever meet anybody who just doesn't think the rules apply to him? You don't want to get that far into a relationship with a guy who struggles this way. You sure don't want to marry him.

10. A spiritual *boy* has to win every argument, has to always have the last word. "You're ugly." "Am not." "Are to." "Am Not." "Are to." Time to put away childish things. And one of them is the pride that drives, "Am not." "Are to." And keeps him away from, "You know, that's really something to think about." Or even better, "You're right. I've never thought about it that way." Or even, "I think we'll have to agree to disagree on that one and get on to just enjoying each other's company."

11. Spiritual boys talk and talk and talk and say angry things that hurt other people. "Likewise, urge the younger men to be self-controlled" (Titus 2:6). And controlling the tongue and the emotions that drive it to dark places is one of the major marks of maturity.

12. Finally, the weekend is recess. Time to play cowboys and Indians with the guys. "I work five days a week, three hours a day. That's enough obligation for any man. Saturday morning's golf, Saturday afternoon's the dune buggy. Sunday's beer and pretzels. Church? Who's got time for church? And visiting her folks? Or kids? Come on! The weekend's too full of the important things. I'll probably have to take a sick day Monday to rest up. I'm entitled!"

Primary to understanding maturity is one's use of time. Time is a gift; you're given time. God gives it, and because He's given it to you to use within the priority scheme set down in His word, how you use it reflects on your walk with Him. Do you use it in a mature way, with an eye on investing in important relationships, or do you use it for self-gratification and boyish endeavors?

One matter of maturity for men is being the spiritual leader in the home. Who initiates spiritual things at home? Is it the man or the woman? If it's the woman, then the man's not a spiritually mature man. He's still a boy spiritually. He's not grown up to maturity yet. Church are full of men who are responders to their wives spiritual initiatives.

I have observed many dating relationships between college students where, if anything spiritual happens, it's because the woman initiates it. Guys seldom suggest a Christian concert, a special function at church, a discipleship retreat, or a spiritual formation book to read. He generally defers to her lead. If that's the case, he may be wonderful, and you may go gaga over his masculine appearance, but he may not have grown up enough to lead you spiritually.

Another key indicator of immaturity is if the man is still acting on youthful sexual desires that control his behavior. Whether pornography or vying for various women's attention, the man behaves like he's still a teenager trying to prove his manhood. All this testosterone spreading tells any perceptive woman that he's just not ready, or may never be ready, for a mature, loving, spiritual long-term relationship.

If a guy is constantly making sexual jokes, or everything he says has some sexual innuendo tagged on the end of it, he's got some growing up to do. If he behaves this way around his friends and around you, he may be enrolled in college but emotionally and spiritually, he's still in junior high. And a boy in junior high is too young for a lasting and healthy relationship.

What, then, are some aspects of spiritual manhood? We've already explored some of the ways a guy will show you he's not mature enough. How might be reveal the opposite, that he is mature enough to handle adulthood and the responsibilities that come with it?

First, maturity levels reveal themselves like a lighthouse beacon in the way you act and react when life goes south on you. I mentioned that the higher the level of maturity, the greater the control over one's words and emotions. For instance, if you're dating a guy who flies around on the highway, screaming angrily at this driver and that, barreling up and around other cars, flipping the drivers off as if he owns the road and others have no right to any part of it, there's a real reason he behaves like that. Instead of driving a Chevy, he belongs on a balloon-tire Schwinn with streamers on the handlebars and a clothes-pinned playing card chirping in the spokes. Take a kid's toys away from him and he wails, screams, and kicks his feet—same as an immature guy who doesn't get his own way on the road. It's the same for the maturity level of women, but their turn will come later. Take a look at yourself and/or the guy you're dating. When life doesn't come at you on your terms, how do you deal with it? How do you act when someone cuts you off in traffic, steals you parking space, goes thirty-five in the fast lane? Some ladies will tell me, "Everything's fine until he gets in a car." He fires back. "The biggest problem is, she won't ride with me anywhere." Well why not? "Because he's going to get us killed. He's an idiot when he gets behind the wheel." Well, that wheel's not the problem. He must grow up enough to know he's not going to benefit his family or anybody else by exploding right there in the driver's seat, or getting involved in a fist fight alongside the road with some other hothead." Then it's got nothing to do with the car, the traffic, or the other hotheads on the road. The problem is, all that acting out is only a symptom of a much larger, all pervasive matters such as unresolved pain, anger, or gross immaturity.

That's not to say that we're all susceptible to getting a little hot under the collar when we're behind the wheel and we're thwarted by some other driver. We can all be pushed to our limits. But maturity and the resulting wisdom step in to calm us down, and bring it all to a safe, sane conclusion. When safe and sane conclusions are not part of your particular scenario, then it's time to take all that immaturity and pent-up rage to our our healer, God, so He and you can be restored and healed.

You may find that the car is just the pressure cooker, the ingredients cooking might be something else altogether. You might be anxious about going home (maybe you don't feel particularly safe there), or about something at work or school. Whatever it is and wherever it occurs—car, work, home—there are good, healthy, uplifting ways to deal with it. Maybe you need help putting something behind you; maybe you need to forgive; maybe to just need to learn to love as God loves you. Take the opportunity of having this behavior pointed out, to deal with it in a mature, godly way. This isn't about right or wrong. It's what you and God are going to do with it.

And the car is just one crucible. Life can turn on you a lot of different ways. You get a pay cut when you can hardly make the rent now. You can't get the class you need for graduation. You break your leg and miss a midterm and the professor laughs when you ask for a makeup. On the co-ed flag football team, a guy beats you out for the starting quarterback position and you just can't get over it. You're not grieving, not taking your time to process what you perceive as the humiliation—so you can't get over it. You are so angry that you want to key his car! That's immaturity. And it says a lot about who you are and where there needs to be growth.

Let's talk about *character* and how maturity is reflected in it. What is character? Simply said, it's *how a person acts when no one is watching*. But only you know what that is. How can a date or prospective spouse tell that? Isn't it like asking a bystander what the crash of a falling tree sounds like when no one's there to hear it? Well, it is, in a way. But what we do in secret is often revealed in how we act among friends or when under severe stress. That's why we suggest you know someone for a long time before you commit to him. People will often loosen up as they get increasingly familiar with you, saying and doing what they may hide around mere acquaintances or strangers. If a person takes on different characteristics when he's with you, he will assume a different persona when you're not around. If that's the case, you have a behavioral chameleon on your hands, someone without character or very little of it. Character is consistency and good character is when someone is consistently, predictably good, not perfect; our maturity has more to do with our direction than our perfection. A man of character doesn't fudge on his timecard, steal copies or supplies from work, or take advantage of a friendship.

If a man does have major, consistent flaws, God can change his character over time, if he's a surrendered child of God. Over time and as we work out our salvation with "fear and trembling," we will grow up spiritually and mature, be one who follows righteousness like that "deer after that water brook." But if you're a guy (or gal) who's college aged nineteen, twenty, twenty-one, or twenty-two years old and you're still cheating on tests and still see work as some kind of free lunch, the maturity or the lack of it is still an issue for you. For instance, not long ago, I had a conversation with a female student. As we talked, she mentioned that her boyfriend, who worked at a coffee shop, was a little light fingered at work. He brought things that belonged to the shop home with him after work. She told me she didn't think this was right. "What does he say when you confront him about this?" I asked her. "Well, he says that no one ever misses the stuff. So who cares?"

Just because people aren't watching or don't immediately feel the effects of your inappropriate action, doesn't morph bad character to good. Just as not getting caught doesn't, either. Although, many believe not getting caught is a good thing. They even make jokes about how they got away with something. It certainly keeps the reputation and the arrest record clean. However, being caught and suffering the humiliation and facing consequences might be what straightens a guy up—matures him in a hurry. God's right there to nudge us back into line and develop our character. Godly conviction of a character flaw, a person's acting upon that conviction in repentance and sorry is a very good sign that the guy is mature. Knowing the Lord isn't enough. I know a lot of immature thirteen-year-olds who know the Lord and even praise God publically. Being mature in the Lord is where you want your guy to be and nowhere else.

None of us are perfect; we all carry emotional and psychological wounds around with us. Some have developed into scars, some are healing, but we all have them. Some of these have resulted from our own spiritual weakness. It takes maturity to recognize that we have those weaknesses, and it takes even more maturity to go through the painful process of nullifying them or turning them into spiritual strengths at times. If a guy refuses to own or take responsibility for, his weaknesses or, worse yet, is unwilling to face the fact that he has any to begin with, he's still in his spiritual adolescence phase.

So when do you find all this out about a guy? I don't know of any dating relationship that didn't sprout from a friendship relationship or any marriage that didn't bloom from dating. You hang out with a lot of people you never become friends with. And you probably have far more friends than you do people out of the friendship pool that you date. Forming friendships takes time. Dating and cultivating an exclusive relationship takes more time. And narrowing down the people you date to the one person you marry takes even more time. And whether you think so or not, you have time. God's given you all the time you need to find the one person on earth to be your lifemate—be patient and trust Him.

So what do you do with all this time? Above all, you're developing your relationship with God; you're working out your salvation with fear and trembling. You're learning about yourself—your likes, dislikes, wounds, who needs to be forgiven, and what you need to let go of your gifts, talents, desires, passions. You're slipping into the place God has for you, a place or a series of places where you'll utilize your gifts and talents and realize your desires and passions. Along the way, you'll meet people—men, women, kids. You'll become acquainted with a great many of them, and out of those acquaintances, you'll develop friendships. Your friends will have similar values. Among them, if you're true to your calling, they'll value the Lord, be—as you are—one of Christ's, one of God's children. Some of these friends will be guys. And from them, you'll learn more about men in general. We're different. Learn about us, what makes us men, the hunter/gatherer in us, the warrior—the good and not so good. Out of that pool of friends, you may find yourself attracted to one or more of them. You enjoy spending time with them, you laugh when you're around them; you seek their strength, their advice, their perspective. Maybe there's the hint of a romantic attraction or more than a hint. You date in a movie, miniature golf, the beach, a party, a concert. Someplace where you get to know the guy more personally—his witness, where he is in his walk with the Lord, if he's a spiritual leader, if he's mature enough for a relationship. And if he's not? You pray for him and hand him back to the Lord for more work. Then you wait for God to open the next door, bring the next opportunity for growth. You've got to have this progression of events in mind. God doesn't want you to settle for less. His choice for you is not an almost fit; it's the best match. And maturity is high on the Lord's list for the guy you marry. If it's not, then you better check your own maturity level.

What about the gal who says, "All this doesn't matter. I'm not married, don't plan to get married very soon. I'm just dating, just having fun." I hope you are having fun. Although dating is serious stuff, having fun is a big part of it. Who wants to date and certainly marry someone you don't have fun with? There's nothing wrong with biding your time, putting yourself in a holding pattern, just having fun. There may be convincing reasons to do that in your life. You might move out of the area sometime in the future. You might want to use all your creative energies toward your studies, getting the job you want, or developing a specific skill before you open yourself up for a long-term relationship. You might want to keep yourself to casual gatherings, to people you only see occasionally and keep your close friends to only a few, and not date at all. In that case, your emotional investment is small, perhaps nonexistent. But if you're kidding yourself or find yourself seeing the same people day after day, gaining emotional and psychological support from certain persons, and if, on the rare day you don't see them, you miss them deeply, then whether you want to admit it or not, the emotional investment is high and probably so because of only one or two people within the group. Also, if you're a gal and one of them is a guy, you would do yourself a big favor to begin factoring into that relationship, the maturity elements we've covered here. While you're doing that, slide yourself back into the whole acquaintance, friendship, dating, and marriage progression so you don't miss something you live to regret.

One of those "something's missing" might to be this: godliness, another sign of spiritual manhood. What is godliness? It's the interest in and attraction to the things and people of God. The guy could be a Christian studies major, an English or physical education major. The definition has nothing to do with academics although it might spawn academic pursuits. It has everything to do with a heartfelt, heart directed interest in God and all that surrounds Him. This Christian is the deer after the water brook (Ps. 42:1). He talks about Christian spiritual things, he wants to be around Christian spiritual things, he feels empty when Christian spiritual things are missing, and he has a desire for God's work. A passion for the church and consistent corporate participation is a matter of spiritual maturity as well.

You say, "Well, I believe in God. I love God. I love Jesus. He's my savior, but I care nothing about the church." One idea doesn't support the other, because the church is the body of Christ. The church, His people, is what Jesus died for. You can't disassociate the two. And one sign of spiritual maturity, of spiritual manhood, is an interest and attraction to the church, its people, and the spiritual activities embodied in it. A mere interest is not enough. In spiritual mature men, the church becomes part of who he is, just as it should be a part of who you are. Both of you should want to invest in spiritual things. Invest in time, energy, money, talent, spiritual gifts, imagination, creativity, and talent, all of which can be transformed into various scriptural activities—individual, group or small group ministries, Bible studies, discipleship, missions, community ministry, children's and teen ministries, and so forth. The depth of participation is often directly proportionate to the level of interest and attraction.

Those who profess faith but seem not to be attracted to the things of God are spiritual boys or carnal Christians. In 1 Corinthians 3, Paul discusses those he would like to address as spiritually mature, but can't. Although he calls them brothers, meaning they are those born from the womb of Christ and identify with faith in Christ, but they act like infants. They are infants in Christ, not grown up yet, which demanded he give them milk and not solid food to chew—simple Christian concepts, not the meat of complexity of the deeper things of God. The carnal Christian is just not mature. But there's no particular chronological age involved here. Not all mature the same way, at the same rate. Some grow very rapidly in spiritual things, while others mature more slowly. The carnal Christian is identified in the scripture as one who still acts in largely carnal ways, like those of the world—thus the term *carnal Christian*. So what does this all mean?

There are four areas where levels of maturity are revealed. The first we'll cover is appearance. How people present themselves is telling about their level of maturity. If you're too concerned about looks, it shows you haven't grown enough to understand the importance of the inner person; externals are far too important to you. How you look defines your identity and feeling of worth as a person. It may also mean that Mom or Dad is still paying for your look. They are springing for the expensive styles and labels and allowing you to be more fashion than budget conscious. Maturity means you've begun to shoulder that responsibility. Now there are more trips to Old Navy and fewer to Nordstrom's. Maturity envelops the wallet. That's not to say you may not need a good suit or a well-made pair of shoes. But utility and need is always weighed against the cost; appropriate takes center stage. Clothes become just clothes. And you also begin to better understand why you wanted to spend so much time on your appearance before, why you wanted to look so manly, bad boy, hot, or very, very cool. Did you think it would further your relationships? Set you apart? Make you more desirable? Make you more a part of the world and what it represents?

I was at the pool one Saturday with my wife, Roxanna, and we overheard some women talking. They were about forty-five, and one of them spoke about this guy who also lives in the complex.

"Oh, my gosh," she exclaimed like a teenager, "he is *so* hot. I hope someday he notices me."

Over the course of fifteen minutes, she said this at least three times, always speaking of the same person. *You're forty-five years old*, I thought. *Forty-five. You're acting like a kid.*" Apparently, she's not married. But she's dating, and instead of looking for someone mature, someone with a good character, someone who'll want her for who she is inside, and someone who will be willing to remain with her through the good and the not so good, her primary sizzle results from the guy looking hot—about an image, not substance.

On the other end of the spectrum, if you're essentially a sloppy ill-kept mess, disheveled, dressed inappropriately, or perhaps dirty, you're saying you just don't care, showing the proper respect means nothing; hygiene and its affects are worthless concepts, the norms of a civilized society don't apply to you. You think as a child thinks. Even employers resist hiring unkempt people. If you ever want to support yourself or a family above the poverty level, you'll want to adjust your appearance to clean, stylish, and appropriate to the occasion.

Mature Christians distance themselves of all the world's influences and find their value and identity in Christ. Their outward appearance is modest and appropriate while being fashionably relevant.

The next maturity characteristic to consider is speech. The Bible has much to say about our speech Jesus laid it on the line. "You brood of vipers! How can you speak good, when you are evil? *For out of the abundance of the heart, the mouth speaks.*" (Matt. 12:34, NIV). One sure sign of what the nature of the heart's abundance is the nature of the jokes a person tells. Are they punctuated by sexual innuendo? Do the jokes give us a good laugh about the overweight or special needs people? Or is his humor sarcastic, negative, or degrading. Is someone's mistake fodder for his funny mill? It could be a sign of immaturity, because that's what humor is in junior high. I know my office, for years, was on the second floor right over the junior high playground. Lunchtime is a boiling sea of seventh grade humor. "Did you see Amber's skanky outfit? She looks so slutty today" or "They are so lame!" I hope you have a higher expectations of verbal maturity for someone you spend time with, someone in whom you invest your heart and possibly your life.

The next beacon that peers deeply into guys' hearts is their list of interests. Where do they spend their spare time and on what? What are their toys? Dune buggies, motorcycles, waverunners, video games. Does he bury himself in football all weekend with his buddies? Snowboard all winter? Boogie board all summer? Have you had to take up something you don't really enjoy, such as Texas Hold'em, just to get on his calendar? Is everything about him? "There's a Nicholas Sparks movie coming out we have to see. She loves him and he dies. You'll love it. What's that face? I don't give you a face like that, ever!"

At the beginning of a relationship, often it's about accommodating. "Okay, he likes football—all weekend he likes football—but in all other ways, he's perfect." However, when the relationship lasts long enough for those first schoolgirl emotions to begin to wane, you want to know if you are high on his list of interests. You want to know if he would take you to the hospital during a playoff game; he would actually take you and not just call you a cab. You want to know you're the one he's interested in above all else, and sometimes, finding that out takes some time. The longer you get to know a guy, the more choices between you and something else he'll have time to make, the more opportunity God has to show you who this guy really is and how deeply he cares for you and his potential for a lasting healthy relationship.

I spoke to a girl who'd dated a guy for two years. "He's a great guy," she told me. "But he makes me crazy. If I want to spend any time with him on a Saturday, I have to ride in his golf cart. If a tornado struck the club house, he wouldn't leave that golf course on Saturday." Will that change after they get married? Probably not. He might say it will. "Then it'll be just you and me, honey. Golf won't mean anything to after we get married." Of course, now and then, we run across an honest guy, and they will make grownup choices after they marry. A guy may say, "When I commit to someone or we get engaged, certainly when we get married, I'll place that person on top. But for now, she's number two or maybe even number three." Just make sure when that commitment comes, you keep watch for the changes. Maturity is about choosing what's important, enduring, and benefiting to others. You want to be that choice.

What, then, does he choose when he has discretionary time? Does he volunteer at a local homeless shelter or head to Mexico to help build a house for somebody? Does he have a heart for ministry or service to others? Giving his time to help his friends and family in their times of need reflects a great deal about what he values most.

Matthew 6:21 puts it this way: "For where your treasure is, there your heart will be also." For that guy on the golf course every Saturday, his treasure was his low golf scores, a low handicap. The question is, What's your treasure and how does having that for a treasure affect your life and your relationships?

Let's talk about one of the most valuable treasures you have. Why? Because everyone has demands upon them—studying, family, work, those intruding elements such as broken cars, needy friends, demanding bosses or professors. And let's not forget God, who wants all of it and deserves all of it. You're pressed. Right now, you're probably thinking about ten other things you should or want to be doing. How a guy spends his time is part of his treasure—his discretionary time. But even his non-discretionary time, we can tell a lot about a person when we look at where he requires himself to spend his time, what he's obligated himself to. We might consider time set aside for homework as non-discretionary. It's time we just have to put in. But the fact that he's set that time aside and requires himself to spend it there tells you a lot about how a man discharges his responsibilities. Often, we think of the time we put into relationships as discretionary. "Let's go to a movie," sounds like the siren call for a lazy afternoon. But if you're going to have a relationship, you need to designate some time to it. Date night, for instance. Couples can become so tied up with work, school, family obligations, and church activities that they have no time for themselves. And they need that time. That's the time when they truly find out if they could spend the rest of their lives with one another. Do they have fun together? What happens when plans crumble, when emergencies arise, when lives bleed over into "couple" time? So discretionary time becomes non-discretionary. But during discretionary time, when he really has nothing else of importance to do, does he call, come over, or want to spend it with you? And does he sometimes make his discretionary time, your discretionary time? "Hey, I suddenly have a couple hours I didn't know I had, what say we do something you want to do and I tag along for fun? Whatever it is, it's on me."

I want to encourage you with Matthew 6:21, "For where your treasure is there your heart will also be." When Jesus identifies our hearts as our treasure chest, he's saying what's treasured up in your heart is what matters most to you. It's our directional center emotionally, and sensually. For instance, when we share our faith, we say we've asked Christ to come into my heart. Or we say, "I love you with all my heart." Valentine's Day is all about hearts, right? And when a relationship is shattered, we say, "They broke my heart." What do we mean by *heart*? What is the heart in this context? Well, we're not discussing the organ, the pumper of blood. Although, the organ has been used in a country western song, "She sorta stomped on my aorta. She mashed that sucker flat." And since we've opened the country western door, there's another that tells us: "I met this girl, I gave her my heart. I love her so much I cut a hole in my mattress so I could see her in the spring." That's a metaphor.

The heart can be understood as the seat of our emotions. If you're a ball player and play a game with passion, giving it all you have, you're said to have played with *heart* or have given it your *whole heart*. When investments are made in our passions, the activities we like. Those things upon which we bestow our interest, those investments come from the heart. So, if you want to know what treasure lies within the heart, look at where your time, talents, and resources are spent. Those are the things that truly reflect our loves and affections.

One reason I love the statement "Where your treasure is, there your heart will also be" is it's so telling. To find out what people really love, look at what they do, listen to what they talk about, make note of where they spend their discretionary time. If they tell you they love you but spend no time with you, then do they truly love you? Or if they tell you they love you but only seem to when you do certain things with them, then they don't love you; they love that other thing just a little more when you're a part of it. Love for them isn't giving to you; it's you giving to them. I don't love you. I love me.

I want to challenge you. Maturity can be recognized. The trick is to want it and recognize it. It takes maturity on your part. It takes you wanting to be with, to do things with, and build a future with a mature guy. I'm a guy's guy. I play all kinds of ball. I hunt and fish. And I love golf. But there was about fifteen years when I played golf only a couple times in all those years. Why? Golf takes a lot of time. I had kids, and taking kids on a golf course is a capital offense (or at least it should be). I was working one or two jobs, and I just didn't have time to take six hours to chase a little white ball around. What spare time I did have, I wanted to spend with my family. Golf was a big treasure in my life. But my family was a much higher priority. This particular choice may be down the road for some of you, but other choices aren't. Now is the time to begin setting mature priorities and have expectations of the same, so when choice of a lifemate does wind its way down the road you're navigating, you'll make a wise one.

The lack of male maturity brings up another issue. Most women don't want to mother their husbands. When the guy is immature, there's no choice. Some guys just need to be parented. They act their age only when Mom raises certain expectations, when Mom (which may be you) encourages or demands that they grow up.

Also, has the guy developed an age appropriate distance from his mom? If a guy gets to be nineteen or older and still calls Mom a couple times a day, seeks her advice before he does just about anything, has her doing his laundry and paying his bills, then he's still being mothered.

I know a thirty-five-year old guy. He's a successful business-man and a very gifted leader in a successful ministry. He's also single, and I think there's a reason. He talks to his mom four times a day. He seeks her guiding hand and still needs her nurture. At thirty-five, he wants a mate, of course, but he hasn't yet cut the cord. If he does find a lady willing to wedge herself into that relationship, she'll quickly find she's his mom-mate at best. She might even find herself total-mom or in competition with Mom. But it's highly unlikely she'll find herself a lifemate only.

Has he ever lived on his own? What's a girl going to think? There they are on a date and between the house salad with ranch dressing and the Chicken Parmesan, Mom calls and then calls a half hour later just to make sure he ordered a somewhat-healthy dessert. "She's watching my diet. Breakfast is raisin bran. Lunch is a tuna sandwich, easy on the mayo. She always puts in a Vlasic pickle—love Vlasic pickles." To which the girl responds, "You still live with your mother?" His brows dip, shocked that she doesn't understand. "Who else will watch my diet?" The girl thinks, *Why don't you watch your own diet?* but says nothing. She just crosses him off her list, if she's an emotionally healthy, mature young woman desiring a spiritual and mature relationship. If she's not, she jumps at the chance and says, "I will. I'm good at that. I'll even give you two pickles. Think of that, two pickles!"

In couples' counseling I've learned women rapidly tire of being mom to their husbands. They also tire of being a combination, a mom-mate. They want to be the mate—only the mate. At first, as an accommodation or because you think it's kind of cute, you might take on the role of parent to the guy you're dating, but whether you think so now, you'll get tired of it very soon. Know what you're getting yourself into.

A final thought: Experience has taught me that most women respect a guy who's willing to stand eye to eye with them and ask for the date, a cup of coffee, or "let me walk you to your next class so we can get to know each other a little." They respect the willingness to take the risk and initiative. They certainly respect it more than the guy who follows them around like a puppy. Puppies are very cute but don't get jobs, provide for their families, or take responsibility for all that comes in a family's life. I see college women banging their heads against very strong brick walls all the time because most guys refuse to be men. And the first test of a man's maturity may be a simple and straightforward, "Let's get a cup of coffee and talk for a while. I'd like to get to know you better."

GIRLS TO WOMEN (ROXANNA GRIMES)

Every girl longs to be loved and loved well for a lifetime. But how does she know when she's found it? How does she know when she has found him—the one that will love her and love her well for a lifetime? She won't know until she is found by the One who loves her perfectly and for eternity. It's more about being than finding.

Every girl's heart is designed to be so hidden in Christ that a boy would have to go through Him in order to get to her. To understand this principle is to understand what it means to be a maturing woman capable of a lasting relationship with a godly man. What does it mean for a girl to be hidden in Christ? Does it mean a girl should be invisible? Is she without a voice? Plain? Absolutely not! She is created by the God of the universe, and He delights in His own creation.

If you are a girl reading this chapter, hear me. He delights in you. Let me say it another way. He had the idea of you. He liked the idea. He liked it so much that He planted you in your mother's womb even knowing there would be difficulties. He pushed you through to where you are today because He is passionate about your existence and your purpose. To be hidden in Christ is to be so identified with Him, that you live, love, move, and have your being driven by the love and value His sacrifice placed on you. He deeply loved His Heavenly Father and so do you.

When a girl considers Christ to be enough for her inner most longings and provider for all her earthly needs no matter how vast they are, she is trusting Him for her very existence and well-being. She believes that He is becoming more real to her than the clothes she wears, yet knows He is the provider of them. She knows the God of the universe is the One who made her, and so, He is her reference point for her mind, heart, will, and how to live, move, be held together through all life's painful events as well as the joyous ones. He did not create her for someone or something else. He did not create her to conform to the things and people of this world. He created her for Himself. She, quite frankly, is the love of His heart. After all, He redeemed her at an extravagant cost. When things in her heart are broke, she knows He can put it back together. When she gets confused, He can heal her mind's thinking. When her body gets sick, He knows what it needs to recover. When she is confronted with an enemy, she knows He is available to take it down.

Being identified with Christ is the only way a girl can be secure and walk in confidence. It is the only way she will ever be loved well and loved for a lifetime. Only God can love a girl perfectly and for eternity. With that being said, it becomes the goal of a secure godly girl to make Jesus her highest affection and all other earthly loves fall under that provision and protection. It is reasonable, when Jesus is the highest affection, for a girl to expect her Father Creator to show her the godly man that is capable of loving her well and loving her for a lifetime. Without Christ as her highest affection and reference point for all other loves, it will be very challenging to recognize him when he comes along.

A girl's insecurity will drive her to seek security and identity in people and relationships, moving Jesus out of his most deserving place. When she seeks to find someone to complete her in any way instead of Jesus, she puts her heart in a dangerous position. Instead of choosing someone through her Jesus filter, she will likely choose someone through her "emptiness" filter. Approaching a lifetime marriage relationship from a point of emptiness will perpetuate a possible lifetime cycle of trying to fill up her heart with God like expectations toward her husband that not even the most holy man can fill. Because he isn't God.

In essence, the eternal and perfect love of God is the only love that completely fills and satisfies. It is the remedy for restlessness and longing in a girl's heart. Furthermore, unless two people come together knowing the love of the Father and seeking that above all, most attempts to love each other will be short-lived and somewhat contaminated with dysfunctional love systems.

In other words, this insecure girl will live a god-dependent life instead of a God-dependent one. A _____ [you fill in the blank] dependent life. People, things, places, begin to temporarily fill her angst. Anything and anyone can fill in that blank. I need to add that many of those blank fillers can be good things, such as volunteering, academics, career, children, houses, possessions, church attendance, Bible studies, etc. These are the blessings and the additions that come as a result of seeking to be known and loved by God first. Matthew 6:33 says, "But seek ye first the kingdom of God, and His righteousness, and all these things shall be added unto you." The first phrase of that verse addresses the search for things that matter to God, the things in His heart. Being filled by and known by the heart of God is the satisfying treasure hunt of a lifetime, an eternity! It's the cake. Everything else is the added stuff, the icing.

When you bake a lovely cake, everyone usually anticipates the icing on the cake. But the icing wouldn't be able to live out its best purpose unless it's put on the cake. The substance is the cake. Eating icing out of the bowl instead of on a piece of cake is like putting sugar into your body without the nutrients to break it down properly. You can't find true satisfaction in all the added things without the substance of God's love to carry the needed nutrition to you and your life.

The goal of a secure and maturing girl is to want Jesus more than she wants anything else. What does it look like when a girl needs to have a relationship with a guy more than she thinks she needs God? What would that look like? Think about some situations that reflect that. Perhaps you can't be apart from somebody for very long, or you freak out because he hasn't called you. And you're insecure because it's after lunch and you haven't heard from him. There may be a lot of reasons, but then when he does call, you're upset! I'm talking about how important to your day is the fact that you haven't heard from him in three hours. Or if on a weekend, a guy plans something apart from you. Let's say on Friday night, he plans something other than a date with you. I don't care what it is, maybe it's something really noteworthy, such as volunteering at the local mission or something like that, and you're all put out because he didn't choose to be with you.

It may be an indicator that you have an unhealthy reliance upon the relationship and a less than healthy reliance upon God. And again, healthy relationships are about spending time together. Healthy relationships need quantity and quality of time. But the foundational test of a lasting relationship is based on the worthiness of the person a girl places as her highest affection. The only one worthy of being in the spot of highest affection is God in Christ Jesus. Not a boy, even the godliest one you can find.

When a girl gives Jesus the highest position in her affection, she is poised for the endurance necessary for being in a lifetime relationship. When the vow days come, and they will, she will have the intimacy with Father God already established to provide the foundation of unconditional love, a lifestyle of forgiveness, and grace for herself and the spouse. But better yet, her heart is poised and ready for the wow days that come because she has honored God first and foremost in her heart.

If He isn't the highest affection, true love which originates with God in the first place will be covered over by her attempts to get someone other than God in God's rightful place in her heart. If a girl doesn't offer herself to be loved by God first, her heart will be noisy and distracted as she frantically searches for the boy she thinks will complete and fulfill her other than God. So, due to the lack of real love being on the throne, fear sets in. The voice of fear can be really loud in a girl's head.

The voice of fear speaks lies such as, " Maybe he didn't call me before noon because he really doesn't love me. Or maybe he didn't include me in his Friday plans because he doesn't care about me as much as I care about him. Or maybe he is interested in somebody else." You see, when your head goes there real quickly, it reflects your fear and insecurity, and the voice you allow to speak the loudest. The only remedy to fear and insecurity is an encounter with the love of God.

Second Timothy 1:7 says, "For God has not given us a spirit of fear, but of power and of love and of a sound mind" (NIV). Fear and insecurity is not from God. When a girl experiences it and is driven by it, it is a clear indicator that she has not begun to allow God through Jesus to reign and rule over her heart and certainly not her circumstances. The only way to peace in our circumstances, especially in romantic relationships, is to give Christ, who *is* peace, the throne of her heart. Whoever is on the throne of a girl's heart will be evident in how she handles her tongue, her budget, but most of all, her love life.

Quiet and Gentle Spirit

Please keep reading. Don't let this subheading keep you from experiencing what I believe is the best kept secret for girls straight from the scripture. And it's not just for the married girl. This is highly valuable to the single girl's heart. I call it a secret, because few girls actually take the time to extract the meaning below the surface. Unfortunately, what God intended to be a blessing to every girl, has seemingly gone underground and considered obscure among women in the kingdom.

What was the first thing that came to your mind when you read *quiet and gentle spirit?* Is it similar to what you were thinking when you read *hidden in Christ?* I know. I can relate. I used to struggle with these concepts as well. I have a strong and opinionated nature and disposition, so I really struggled with these until I had an encounter with the love of God after many years of walking with Him.

It wasn't until I reached a burning out in my life, that I was ready to encounter this love. I had lived my whole life rooted in a lie. That lie was, "You are a burden. Your adoptive parents loved you because it was the right thing to do. It was their duty as family members to take you in when you were abandoned by your biological parents." So, in all my encounters with the Lord, from a young child to a grown woman, my filter of love was that of dutiful love. All my God experiences came to me through that same filter. Therefore, I believed God loved me because it was His duty. After all, I am His creation; of course, He has to love me.

Every step I took in my Christian walk was passed through that filter. You can see where I'm going. My entire life became dutiful. Discipline. Knowledge. Work. Faithfulness. Until one day, I just ran out. I couldn't keep up with the expectations of a life filled with Christian duty. Something had to give. I was angry and called it righteous. I felt guilty and called it conviction. I had put up walls and called them boundaries. One day, I just began crying and I couldn't stop.

In my brokenness, the love of God met me. This level of brokenness ushered in a new layer of surrender and letting go. I had many situations and relationships in my life that were hard, and I had come to see I couldn't do anything about them. Over a period of about a week, I continued weeping and confessing, asking forgiveness, and began a real conversation with Jesus that led me to a very simple but profound place in the Bible. "He brought me out into a broad place; He delivered me because he delighted in me" (Ps. 18:19, NIV).

What? God delights in *me*? I never knew. Delight sounds and feels very different from duty. Then I read Zephaniah 3:17, "The Lord your God in your midst, the Mighty One will save; He will rejoice over you with gladness, He will quiet you with His love; He will rejoice over you with singing" (NIV). The deep love of God is experienced through the sweet comforter that God sent to us—the Holy Spirit. But He is a gentleman and only has access to the places we open up to Him. When I got to the end of my rope, I opened up to Him through surrender and confession of my own dutiful love. This opened the door for His love to finally reach my entire soul and flood every crack and crevice and empty place. I like to call it liquid love.

Upon encountering the deep love of God, I came to understand that the Father, the One who created me, could see me. It was as though His very heart poured out toward me in my brokenness and if anyone could see into the spiritual realm, could see I had been identified from heaven as His very own. I had been identified as precious and of a very high value. This identification upon me quieted my heart. I knew I wasn't just another child of God among many. I was one. I was His. I was loved. Almost immediately, at least in its first layers, I stopped wondering what other people were thinking around me. I stopped thinking about whether people really loved me or liked me very much. I knew I was found and loved and delighted in.

My husband told me I had a considerable change in my disposition. Because God's love repositioned me. He lifted my head to show me He saw me and then poured His liquid love directly into my heart.

Submission and Trust

As I was writing this chapter, I received a get-well card from a dear woman named Kay. The front of the card contained prose by Max Lucado: "When Jesus says, 'You are worth more than many sparrows,' trust Him." Only women who are secure in the love and identification of Jesus can fully trust Him throughout life's trials and complicated relationships. His unconditional love helps her to remember that no matter what happens in the earthly experience, His love and care looks after her best interests. He takes care of His children. It is extremely important for a girl to know and trust the One who had the idea of her, saw fit for her to be born, and who is passionate about her purpose and existence. Believing and acceptance of this fact is the foundation for her to be able to live in submission to God first and then her husband.

Let's look at a most important but often controversial passage in the Bible—1 Peter 3.

> Wives, likewise, be submissive to your own husbands, that even if some do not obey the word, they without a word, may be won by the conduct of their wives, when they observe your chaste conduct. Do not let your adorning be external-the braiding of hair and the putting on of gold jewelry, or the clothing you wear- but let your adorning be the hidden person of the heart and the imperishable beauty of a gentle and quiet spirit, which in God's sign is very precious. For this is how the holy women who hoped in God used to adorn themselves, but submitting to their own husbands.
>
> 1 Peter 3:1–5 (ESV)

If a girl hasn't learned to be submissive to God who is perfect and loves her perfectly, how will she learn to be submissive to a man who is going to fall short on more than one occasion throughout her lifetime? Let's break some truths down and bring them into this century concerning chaste conduct.

- *External Adornment.* A girl who is quieted by God's love is supremely aware she is beautifully designed and has intrinsic value that cannot be taken away.

  She doesn't rely on outward adorning of fashion, make-up, and hair to establish her security and approval. I love being a girl! I love to get dressed in the morning, apply simple make-up on most days, and I love jewelry! But the key word is *rely.* My sense of value became identified by my highest affection, which no longer existed in worrying about what people thought of me when they saw me. I began to dress and look at myself not in a regular mirror, but instead, the mirror image God impressed on my heart when He showed me His love and design of me. I love standing at my closet with His pure delight hovering, and asking, "What shall we wear today?" The former decision process involved looking at who was on my calendar that day, what would my mother think, what would my best friend think, and would my kids be embarrassed or proud! The heart that's quieted by His love grows to select things to present herself attractively, but the drive behind the selections are not to find identity or value.

- *Hidden Person.* A girl quieted by God's love has an inner peace that enables her to have a gentle spirit. She has no fear of outcomes, so she can resist the temptation to control and take things into her own hands to get her needs met.

  A secure girl trusts God more than her boyfriend or husband because He has the highest place of affection and is found to be worthy of her trust. Husbands and boyfriends make mistakes, have bad days at work, get moody, and can't predict and meet our every need. She can change and be gentle, because she has submitted to and been gently carried by Father God, her highest affection. He loves to carry her in lonely places to filling her where no man's abilities can. Whatever fills her hidden *inner* person pours out of her *outer* visible person. So, if Father God fills her, His very nature will begin to pour out of her. Any slight of treatment becomes another blessed opportunity to forgive. And this strength does not afford her the life of a doormat but the life of a beautiful pillar anchored to the heart of God and positioned for hearty human intimacy.

- *Imperishable Beauty.* You get what you attract. Just because a godly single girl stands before a pastor and a church filled with friends and family to say marriage vows doesn't mean she is prepared to be submissive. Becoming a woman who is secure enough to be submissive to her husband is founded upon the principle of becoming a secure girl first.

When a godly single girl has found a guy to marry, it doesn't mean it's the right thing to do. The one question I rarely hear single girls talking about before they marry is whether or not the guy they found is going to lay down his life for her.

What godly girl has a problem submitting to a guy who has proven through time and character that he is willing and able to throw himself in front of a bus for her? Well, okay, maybe it won't be a bus, but how about the relationship with his mommy? Will he lay that down for you? Or how about big boy toys and becoming a golf widow? Will he lay down his life for you?

Guy laid down his life for me over and over and over throughout these twenty-eight years. For years, I wore the heaviness of a broken heart for past decisions as well as the decisions of people I loved. All the while, he quietly and prayerfully believed I would heal, making more room for him in my heart. The day came when heaviness left my heart, and when I looked up, I saw a patient, kind, sacrificial man who had quietly laid down his life. And never brings it up.

Single girls, you get what you attract. If you find yourself submitting to a boyfriend out of insecurity, you will likely attract someone who will try to control you or take advantage of your compliance. Honestly, that's what that kind of submission is. Compliance in order to get your needs met. But if you are secure, you will attract a godly guy who is willing to lay down his life for you because of the anticipated incorruptible beauty that will come. He knows you aren't dependent on him for approval and value, and he is attracted to the kind of strength that submits out of respect for the Lord and for him.

Imperishable beauty is birthed in a godly girl when God's love and identity fastens her down. She becomes immoveable to the culture's swinging values and opinions on beauty. She becomes untainted by the drama and gossip that girls often get sucked into out of a need to feel better about themselves. She doesn't need to prove herself to God, to her boyfriend or husband, to her best friend. She only needs to present herself to the highest person of affection—Jesus Christ—where she is found over and over to be loved, accepted, and valued. Her spirit, when filled with that, works its way out of her through sparkling eyes, an easy smile, and a laugh at the future. This incorruptible beauty could not be stolen, even if the worst accident overtook her physical beauty. Incorruptible beauty is born of incorruptible love, and those are the elements that form a quiet and gentle spirit, which is very precious in the sight of God and to a godly man. Hair, clothes, make-up, and styles change. Peace, love, trust, and connection with Father God and your husband don't. Seeking to imbibe your heart in the presence of God transmits his very nature into the fabric of your inner girl. Garments made of fabric will fade, shrink, and wear out. Jewelry will tarnish. His garments of love, redemption, purity, peace, and joy last forever and in fact usher us right into the presence of His face in eternity. Incorruptible beauty comes as a result of knowing incorruptible beauty.

Young girl or young woman, declare today who and what your highest affection is and remove it from its dangerous position in your heart. Replace it with the One who had the very idea of you and liked it so much He planted you in your mother's womb. He saw fit to push you through to get here, even knowing you would encounter pain and difficulty, because He is passionate about your existence and purpose. He is worthy of being your highest affection and will lead you to the man who is very attracted to your needing God more than you need Him.

TRANSPARENCY

Let's focus on transparency, which, we will see, has everything to do with the issue of experiencing lasting and healthy relationships. Transparency is letting others see what's inside of us. The introduction of this text discussed the key question posed in Thomas's book *The Sacred Marriage*: What is the real purpose of relationships? He answers this question by asserting the primary purpose of all of life, and therefore, the relationships that inhabit it is the pursuit of holiness rather than personal happiness. He seems to be right. When we study scripture, we find that God refrains from promising any of us personal happiness. And you can see why, especially when it comes to relationships. When one person gets what he wants, the other may not.

For instance, my sweet wife, Roxanna and I enjoy giving each other foot rubs. They're really amazing. And we've found some great reflexology places in the neighborhood. Twenty bucks gets you an hour foot massage, head massage, neck massage. *Incredible!* The critical matter between us at home is who gets to go first or rather, last. If you go last, you get to take a little nap while you get your feet rubbed—a fun little bonus, to be sure, a bonus we both can't receive. The reality is, personal happiness is many times at the expense of somebody else. In dating and marriage, you may experience these choices often. Just try to pick a movie you both enjoy. That's not to say there isn't happiness associated with the Christian life, but nowhere are we promised a constant or even a frequent stream of it. Our joy is knowing and trusting God and seeing His love for us manifested in our lives, happiness is a bonus. Happiness is often about preference.

As mentioned in the introduction, the Bible is fairly silent on happiness; it has a lot to say about holiness. For instance, Peter tells us, "Be therefore holy because I am holy" (1 Pet. 1:16). Let's open the subject of holiness by exploring difficult relationships. May I preface our discussion, though, by this foundational tip: in the quest to be holy like Peter was, don't find someone to spend most of your time with just to make your life miserable. Don't date the biggest schmuck in the world so you learn more love, joy, peace, patience, kindness, goodness, faithfulness, gentleness, and self-control and, in doing so, get closer to God—not that God might not allow a situation like that for that very purpose but to put yourself there seems a bit masochistic.

But you don't have to purposely try to bring yourself pain to suffer through it now and again. Difficulties occur in relationships. You can't foresee them; situations arise and *bam!* You are up to your ears in pain and sorrow. Since most people are looking toward or in the big lifelong relationship—marriage—we want to minimize all the *bams* we can. One way to do that is to use other relationships and the difficulties they can bring as a training ground; let your employer and roommate relationship tutor you a little. One thing you'll learn right away is life isn't always on your terms. The best laid plans often crumble right before your eyes and you end up following someone through the swamp instead of leading them over dry land. Who on earth has not had a difficult roommate scenario?

The nice way of describing it is the *roommate from hell.* Or if not the roommate, you fill in the blank. It could be the cousin, brother, sister, or drycleaner. When you come in contact with someone who fits the description, do you want to escape, or figure God has something to teach you here and seek Him in the difficult situation? "I want to rip my hair out by my brown roots, but maybe I should stay and learn from the process." My decision to stay became one of my first large-scale relationship tutors. A woman I worked with and her husband were friends of mine. We'd play tennis and just hang out. He was a pastor and to supplement their income, she worked in the campus front office where I was the director. Her name was Debbie and was a fun person to be around—lots of laughter and sparkling conversation. But when it came to work, we were very different. I was new to the office, had been there only a few weeks, and usually arrived between eight-thirty to nine. This particular morning, I showed up about eight-thirty, maybe just a little earlier than before. There she was, television on her desk, curlers in her hair, painting her finger nails. I was stunned. I guess her previous boss allowed it to get this way, I'm not sure.

"Debbie," I said, "let me understand. You come to work to get ready for work?"

"No one's ever here this time of day. It won't be a problem, will it?"

"It is a problem. First of all, *I'm* here. I expect you get ready for work before you actually get to work before you're on the clock."

I think at this point she actually turned the TV sound just a bit down and said, "Well, things are kind of slow in the morning."

"Well, if things are so slow that you can't find work to do, then you don't need to be here," I said. And as this exchange unfolded, all I could think was, *Lord, this makes me crazy. This is the stuff workplace violence is made from.*

I wanted to fire her on the spot, poke an authoritative finger right at her nose, watch her eyes cross as she sees it approach, and then send her home. But because I had a relationship with her husband, a close friend of mine, I figured it best not to fire her, but I did want to shoot her. But having neither shotgun nor crossbow handy, though, I just stepped back. God was teaching me a not-so-pleasant but extremely important lesson about difficult, long-term relationships, a lesson I would not have invited but truly came to value. Sometimes, God wants to change us while we remain in the relationship, the relationship become

God's change agent. The relationship is meant to remain with a different you in it. If you commit yourself to someone for life and you find yourself in difficult times, that's an extremely important factor to consider and pray out.

Now what does *transparency* have to do with any of this? We already discussed the concept of mine, yours, and ours. Into any present relationship, we bring more than just our sparkling personalities. We bring all our past relationship experiences—our family turmoil, the resulting scars and hurts, lessons we may have learned poorly, strategies that do more harm than good, and so forth. What comes to mind when you hear the term *transparency* in the context of relationships? Any synonymous spring up. For instance, *genuine* or *real*, maybe *authentic*.

Here's another—intimacy. It is essential in all close personal relationships. All of us have thoughts, fears, painful experiences, failures, moments in our lives we want to keep away from the prying eyes of those we don't trust. We keep those things closed up in the deepest part of us. Intimacy opens that safe and reveals some, maybe even all, of its contents to those we would trust. When it comes to long-term, loving relationships particularly the marriage relationship, intimacy is vital. It's important we not only see what transpires on the outside but know there's a lot percolating on the inside as well.

Most men by their nature are not the most emotionally and verbally revealing creatures in the world. Anyone ever experience that? Not to pick on men, because I fall into that category. If you are a man and you are offended by my assessment, just stop reading and call a waambluance! I'm not the most revealing person by nature either. Meaning, I'll have thoughts, I'll have feelings, and I'll have emotions. There's a lot of stuff though that I don't show on the outside. But if you're going to have a healthy intimate relationship with someone that will last most, if not all, your life, you have to open up at the very beginning. You have to disclose at least a good bit of what's going on inside. Long-term, healthy relationships require transparency, or intimacy. They go hand in hand. You can't have honesty and intimacy—closeness—without transparency. Now a few examples.

I grew up in a family that didn't see Dad around very much. My mom and dad divorced when I was young, which had me living alone with my dad for quite a while. Then he remarried, and I ended up living in different cities year by year. As a result, one issue brought into adulthood was the inability to trust people, particularly when the stakes were high. The risks were very high for me when Roxanna and I started dating. My lack of trust translated in my inability to ask people for help. Even in the smallest things. Case in point: while driving one day with Roxanna, I reached around searching for a stick of gum. Gum's important, we all know that. So while I'm tooling down the 405 going about 80, I find the pack of gum. I do the best I can to hold onto the steering wheel with my knees while I work at opening that pack of gum, getting the little strip that goes around the pack to tear off the wrapper, work the pack open, and get a stick of the precious gum, all while putting our lives in danger.

And I wouldn't ask for help. All I had to say was, "Roxanna, open this, please." She, on the other hand, seeing death approaching from all sides, says, "I can get that for you." To which I responded in my firmest, gum-retrieving voice, "If a human being can't drive a car and open gum at the same time, they shouldn't be driving a car." Actually, they shouldn't be in either case.

She then said, in that counselor's voice I've learned to truly love and appreciate, "It's not that you can't, the issue is will you let somebody help you." She had uncovered in me a real relationship issue. Oh, if there'd only been one. But there were many, just as you have many; everyone has many. When we come to a relationship, we never come empty handed. You bring some, your partner brings some, and some mix when they meet to create a whole new set. We will discuss in chapter eight relationships have many dimensions, your problems, and our problems—yours, mine, and ours. That being true, it's good that you make an assessment as best you're able of what your liabilities are. Then when you come to a relationship, you lay them out before the other person. In that way your relationships are transparent about assets, liabilities, and potential struggles. If people aren't willing to be honest and open—transparent—with you about their struggles, they may not be honest with themselves. Intimacy, at least the strong potential of it, can only come with some degree of transparency, of openness.

I have counseled several couples who, after five or six years of marriage, found themselves struggling with physical intimacy. After some exploration, it was discovered that one partner had been sexually abused as a child. Although they tried to engage in physical intimacy in the beginning of the marriage, after years of emotional turmoil, they just gave up and were now held an emotional and physical prisoner by that horrible abuse. Don't you think that information would be important, even critical, to the other partner? Isn't that something you should know before you marry someone? If for no other reason but to be a part of the process by which God brings healing, forgiveness, and redemption.

You can't have intimacy—physical, emotional, psychological—without some vulnerability and transparency in a relationship. Now that you know that, I'm sure you will want to run out and let everyone have a peak into the window of your soul. No. Probably not. There are reasons why we aren't more transparent in relationships. Let's explore what some of those reasons might be.

Let's start with *fear* of what people will think. Fear that if I open up, you won't want me around anymore, you won't look at me the same way, or see me in the same light. I'll become a weak liability in your eyes. Fear controls much of our lives. Some of it is healthy, such as fear of walking through town late at night, fear of driving while one opens a pack of gum, fear of hugging a polar bear—this last one is mentioned because of a YouTube video I watched. A woman in Australia decided nothing would make her day more than to have a warm, fuzzy, huggy moment with a polar bear she saw at the zoo. To this noble end, she climbed over the fence, leapt into the moat surrounding the enclosure, swam over to where the polar bear waited and guess what? The polar bear mauled her. Thankfully, the bear didn't kill her. But he didn't hug her, either. A little fear would have been a good thing for our Australian fence climber.

Most fears, though, aren't so healthy. Fear of being you, fear of asking for help that brings me to the acronym for fear. FEAR—False Evidence that Appears Real. For instance, it's night, no moon, and dark outside. You hear a noise out there and are afraid to investigate because you're sure there's something bad out there. Why? You watch scary movies and that's their plot. The danger outside appears real and feels real, but it's based on false evidence. A noise is far more likely to be benign. If you fear sharing something important inside you with someone important in your life because honesty and transparency expose you to rejection, even though the threat appears real, it evaporates when you realize that even if they do reject you, they weren't who you thought they were either. Being without them is best for your future.

But just how open, honest, and transparent are you, and do these characteristics change depending on the relationship and where you are in a relationship? Do you want to expose insanity in the family on the first date? Not likely. But when is it appropriate to disclose what? As a rule, if the relationship is long term, when the issue matters, it's time to disclose and work through it. For example, if your boyfriend loves glider soaring and he invites you to go up with him but you're deathly afraid of being even a few feet off terra firma, it's time to tell him. But if a friend with whom you have no romantic involvement invites you soaring, you might just tell him you have other plans, such as survival. It may be none of his business why you really prefer to remain earth-bound. Or if your girlfriend starts to talk about marriage and you love it when she does, but you know you have issues concerning commitment, it's time to discuss it. Let's say your parents were divorced and both left you largely to fend for yourself. As a result, deep inside you worry about keeping a lifelong commitment and believing the commitment made by someone else will last. Now that you're faced with one, you need to come clean, and if it looks like your potential fiancé is willing to work with you to overcome the issue, get to work to neutralize the issue in your life. But if someone you've dated only a few times initiates the commitment discussion, you might just become vague and "noncommittal." The key to this approach is to understand the nature of your relationship. Let's take a look at how we go about doing that.

First you start by defining the relationship. And for this discussion, let's narrow our focus to the romantic relationship. Let's say you're on the cusp of going exclusive. There's no ring, no engagement, and maybe you haven't even met the parents yet, but you've decided you're not going to pursue anyone else—for the time being—and if that works out, maybe forever. Is it time for full disclosure? At an appropriate level, yes. If you're going exclusive, are there issues in your past that might influence your commitment, make it stronger than is appropriate, or hinder its development? Do you have anger issues that an exclusive arrangement might aggravate? Introspections like these make sense at this juncture.

At engagement time, when you're looking at a lifetime as "one flesh," the issues of life that may effect that commitment broaden, and with it, the range of disclosure. To lessen the embarrassment of a broken engagement, we might want to move into full disclosure mode before rings are bought and knees are bent. How do you know when the engagement's blossoming just beyond the bend? You'll know. Despite all the YouTube videos, nobody is completely surprised when the ring comes out, particularly assuming traditional trajectories. The guy, instinct, intuition, and hopefully, the Holy Spirit will tell you when it's time to have these conversations. "You do know, I want to have at least three kids, Lord willing?" or "I really don't want to live in an apartment, even for a little while. My folks broke up because of an apartment. Too many people, too close. We really do need to find a house with a big yard, a place for our three kids—which I want right off—to play. And I love big dogs. Don't you?" Or more seriously, "When I was ten, I was molested by a neighbor boy. We need to talk about how this might affect our future." However, the conversation goes or whatever the topics, there must be transparency concerning the important matters down the road that will impact the relationship. Everybody has them. It's not a matter of "if" you'll have that conversation but "when." Will it be at the appropriate time when passions are at a minimum and you and your prospective fiancé can reason things out? Or will they be in the heat of battle, when passion and rage push reason aside. In either case, we are the products of God's design additionally fashioned by the path He's placed us on. That path had victories and defeats, high points, and stumbling blocks. Both have left their mark and will eventually affect our relationships. Some are subtle; others, such as molestation or prison stay, are not.

You and your prospective lifemate want to know all this at the appropriate time, when the level of decision that's being made could potentially be affected. For instance, my parents went through a horrible divorce and it impacted me emotionally and ever since has colored my relationship decisions. The scars weren't catastrophic, but they were important. By sharing the fact with my then-fiancé, it gave her a heads up, a framework to better understand where I was coming from. If I behaved is a way that seemed to emanate from that hurt, she could react accordingly with empathy, understanding, and loving acknowledgement. Rather than have to react when the scars from that personal ordeal push her into some kind of emotional corner, when understanding is replaced by a strong sense of survival. Such a moment presents a far less advantageous footing for a relationship. How full or detailed, then, does the disclosure have to be?

It's all about intimacy but details and timing matter tremendously. Because there are the broad strokes and there are the narrow strokes. And I don't think it's important with someone we're dating or even our lifemate that the details are recants of everything. Significant matters of our past are not confined to our past. Major life experiences often impact our present and future relationships. In order to have genuine intimacy, both need to know, at least in broad strokes, the significant events of the past. The ones with the past must understand the parts of them that influence their thoughts and behaviors, while the other must empathize and see their partner through the prism of their past. That, prism, however, is tinted and formed by the broad strokes of the past, not the details. If there has been molestation, the fact of it may be enough. There may be no need for the details of it. Many couples discover one or both of them have experienced physical or emotional abuse, sometimes even sexual abuse. It may be enough to know a general description about painful experiences. That basic knowledge may keep your relationship steady when an emotion created in the past erupts in the present.

Your readiness to share the details of a past trauma will often depend on how safe you feel in that particular relationship. When you're first learning about one another, you won't share many or any details. Later, if and when you feel safer emotionally, some details may surface, which, at times, can make things more difficult. Even so, not being transparent, not presenting even the broad strokes may create even a bigger problem. Behaviors that could be easily explained and understood now become behaviors that seem erratic, maybe even threatening. Foundations can be shaken, even to the point of crumbling.

So, as we talk about a relationship moving from the first cup of coffee, to the first real date, to the moment of exclusivity, to meeting the parents, to engagement, to the altar, we also talk about an increased level of transparency. Then, as the marriage progresses from honeymoon, to children, to empty nest, transparency may also increase not so much in disclosure but perhaps, if need be, in finer strokes. Not to stave off the deterioration of your commitment to one another, but to increase the understanding and empathy that forms the cement of a relationship.

Of course, the worry is that disclosure may cause the one hearing it to bolt, to throw hands in the air and refuse to go on. "You're just going to be too high maintenance. I'm outta here." But the real concern should be for your faithfulness to the relationship and the desire to build a "safe harbor" for your mate. If one day he or she finds out you've withheld important information, information vital to the success of the relationship and for his or her emotional wellbeing, how safe will your spouse feel? How much trust would you expect him or her to have? How much more of an investment would you expect your spouse to be willing to make?

We once counseled a young man who had a long history—several years of severe sexual problems. The issues caused him, as a single guy, to have many sexual encounters. When he finally met the right girl and married, though, his promiscuity stopped. He remained faithful. However, he never told his wife that he was quite so sexually active before he'd met her. He figured it didn't matter. It did. They were constantly running into these old flames. After the fifth or sixth woman his wife met who'd been intimate with her husband at one time, the experience began to wear thin. "You told me there were some, but this is more than some. How can I possibly trust you after you misled me like that?"

Disclosure has to be commensurate with the level of intimacy and the expectations of the relationship. There has to be equality between how deep your commitment is and how deep you allow your partner to see. That said, there are ways to misuse transparency. One of them we've touched on when we discussed codependence and independence. If within a relationship, unhealthy patterns develop in an effort to keep a relationship going or push a relationship to the next level, then the relationship falls into the category of codependent. Transparency can sometimes be used to do that. In my single days, there were times when I disclosed an element of my past to a woman because I thought both the disclosure and what I was disclosing would bring us closer, make the relationship I longed for more resilient, warmer, more satisfying to my "needs." Using transparency that way is grossly inappropriate. Vulnerability is to be sincere and honest, without self-serving motives. God is the satisfier of our needs—ever faithful,

145

ever present, always good to us. We know God is the only one who will make us whole, content, joyful, and satisfied. When that *wholeness principle* is in place, you know how much disclosure and who you disclose it to.

Roxanna and I had been dating for a few weeks when she disclosed that she didn't walk with God during college. She began by sharing the broad strokes about her life and decisions that resulted in painful consequences. We were both looking to the Lord to guide our relationship, which He did. But there came a time when the broad strokes became finer. She felt that she was being dishonest if she didn't begin painting with those finer strokes. She shared her heart and bore her soul to me. After we talked, I became even more endeared to her. She later told me she was glad that she married a man whose hope was in God, not in who I'd been and that God used those precious transparent moments to further heal her.

The foundation to all this is our intimacy and attachment to God. Transparency isn't used to *attract* attachment or *test* attachment, which, in turn, fosters an inappropriate, unhealthy, ungodly form of attachment. It is part of the progression of intimacy inherent in a healthy, godly relationship. As such, it's a heart issue. Caution and wisdom are needed to guide what is revealed and when in a healthy relationship. The bottom line is who we are today is to be a reflection of God's redemptive work in our lives. Satan would love to take all our past sins and all the hurt they inspired and translate them all into unhealthy needs that boil inside of us, demanding satisfaction from even more sin, more hurt, and more and more of that vicious cycle. Our transparency in relationships and honesty with ourselves foils the destructive nature of sin. We take our sinful, unhealthy pasts, turn them over to the mercy and grace of our Savior, and He uses all of it to strengthen and bring intimacy to our present and future relationships.

There is another fear that keeps us from transparency—fear of condemnation. Transparency will keep me from being accepted.

You will be judged and found wanting. There's only one judge and that's Christ, and if you are in Him, there is no condemnation. "He who is without sin, cast the first stone." If your move toward broad stroke transparency causes the hearer to gasp in horror and condemn you, he or she isn't a safe companion for life.

Part of this perspective, at least, is reflected in scripture. Let's look at Luke 7:37–39.

> A woman in that town who lived a sinful life learned that Jesus was eating at the Pharisee's house, so she came there with an alabaster jar of perfume. As she stood behind him at his feet weeping, she began to wet his feet with her tears. Then she wiped them with her hair, kissed them and poured perfume on them. When the Pharisee who had invited him saw this, he said to himself, "If this man were a prophet, he would know who is touching him and what kind of woman she is—that she is a sinner (NIV).

How then did the Lord respond? With the parable that teaches that one who is forgiven much loves much. And finally, this in verses 44–47.

> Then he turned toward the woman and said to Simon "Do you see this woman? I came into your house. You did not give me any water for my feet, but she wet my feet with her tears and wiped them with her hair. You did not give me a kiss, but this woman, from the time I entered, has not stopped kissing my feet. You did not put oil on my head, but she has poured perfume on my feet. Therefore, I tell you, her many sins have been forgiven—as her great love has shown. But whoever has been forgiven little loves little (NIV).

What do you think he meant by that? When we become aware of the depth of our own sin, the sins of others fade. We generally look past them or our emotions about the sinner turns increasingly to sadness; we know what sin bring with it. This all comes from the knowledge of what you've done before God instead of consternation about what others have done. That was the whole point. He looked past it saying, you know what, if you're going to look at sin, don't look at somebody else's sin. Look at your own. As the Lord tells us forcefully in Matthew 7:4–6, "How can you say to your brother, 'Let me remove the speck from your eye'; and look, a plank *is* in your own eye? Hypocrite! First remove the plank from your own eye, and then you will see clearly to remove the speck from your brother's eye" (NIV). Because, when it comes to sin, our focus is primarily on our own. When she told me about her background, in comparison, it didn't come close to mine. I grew up in a non-Christian home; none of my family came from Christian backgrounds, so my upbringing bore no relationship to a Christian's childhood. When I heard about her struggles although they were vital to her and vital in fashioning her into the godly woman she is today, they didn't seem like any big thing to me when compared to the path I walked. Every stop she'd made along the way, I made a stop like it. My experience with God and hers were not that different.

And the Lord forgave me for all of it. To look judgmentally at sins someone else has committed is called *self-righteousness*. "I'm not so bad. Look at what that person's done." Or, worse yet, "What a miserable human being! I'd never do anything like that." Sounds terrible, but this sort of condemnation/self-righteousness is easy to fall into. And when people fall into it when their partners begin to share some of their struggles of life, they immediately feel judged, and judgment brings silence and distance—certainly not the intimacy long-term relationships are built on.

Just to put a finer point on it, when a relationship evolves into exclusivity and you've found the one with which you want to begin building the foundation of a permanent relationship, then you begin to share more details. There are probably many ways to define what that moment is, but we all know in our hearts when it's arrived. The thought of going out with someone else just doesn't sound like what you want to do. It's not that you have consciously stopped looking; it's just that your focus is fixed. No one else comes into view. That's when it's important to begin the sharing process—a little at a time, but over time, a lot. And just as you begin to share, when your partner begins to share, you're not there to judge. You're there to see them as a brother or sister in Christ whose sins are forgiven just as yours have been. You're not here to judge but to love (as siblings in Christ), support your partner in his or her Christian walk, and be aware of God's work in your own life. Get about removing those planks in your own eyes before you concern yourself with the speck in your partner's eye.

This is important stuff, perhaps one of the most important issues in your adult life. So much of your happiness depends on your relationship with your spouse. That means that the relationship preceding marriage is important as well. Healthy and lasting relationships are built upon honesty and trust. Transparency is a fundamental element to both. The importance of transparency means that we need to be good at it. We need to be as wise, grounded, understanding, and schooled in loving as Christ is perfect in His love for us.

To achieve this level of proficiency in transparency, we need to practice it, and as we practice, rely on the God and His grace. Many who take advantage of this book will be in their early twenties. That said, when the reader looks back at being sixteen, that phase of life seems quite different—night and day different—yet it wasn't all that long ago. We're only talking about four or five years, yet that age may seem eons from the age in which your now find yourselves. As are relationships.

In junior high, you pass notes around or text a friend. "Does Pam like me?" "Don't you think Brad's cute? But he's got brown eyes. I could never life a guy with the same color eyes as my dog." "I heard Mark and Mary broke up." And so it goes. Our lives were hesitant, self-absorbed, equal blends of comedy and tragedy.

Wisdom had very little to do with our daily lives and particularly, when it came to romance. Of course, a lot of us, particularly the guys, still have a lot of insecurities that drive them to behave today as they did back then. They won't even consider asking a girl out unless they've first have gotten the right answer from two or three of her friends.

Complex, isn't it? And that complexity has changed over time with each new generation. In the ancient world, choosing a mate wasn't an individual process. Families got involved, even match-makers and chaperones. It was well understood that often there were elements to a lifelong match that needed input from dispassionate sources. Not so much anymore. We not only assume, but insist upon the notion that we know best. Our judgment in matters of love is fallible.

As long as you seek God's leadership and consider His ways into the decision, I don't think there's anything wrong with you being the only other one involved. But if you are going to take on the mate selection process as an individual sport, you do need to realize that practice is important. But practice does not in and of itself lead to proficiency.

Have you ever taken part in a sport? Practice is the name of the game. But so is coaching. The coach makes sure you're practicing the right things, that your stance is correct, your swing is perfect, your emotional footing is sound, and so it is with practicing the fine art of relationship making and sustaining. God is our absolute life director. The Bible reveals His designs for relationships. And just like any difficult sport (and there are none more difficult than this one) the athlete makes a lot of mistakes, errors in judgment and experiences losses while growing.

For our purposes here, let's focus on the fundamental issues of relationships. At the top of the list is communication, a subject we'll deal with more in the last chapter of this book. But for now, let's just state: unless you learn the art of effective communication, there will be a myriad of miscommunications—incessant frustrations about what you're trying to say, what you mean by what you say, what they hear when you say it, and just as importantly, what you actually hear when they respond.

When it comes to building the scaffolding that supports a lasting relationship, we all go through those long periods usually lasting 'til death of trial and error. What works and what doesn't. What terrifies and what comforts. What's funny and what's not. What expresses love and what reveals indifference. What she wants to hear and what he doesn't. What tickles and what hurts. And if we're serious about our lessons and truly want to become the person someone will want to stick with for the best part of a century, we learn. Just as a golfer eventually learns the proper swing, a rider learns how to sit on a horse, or a French chef learns how to make a soufflé, we eventually learn how to make a lasting relationship last. We eventually learn what God really means by love, forgiveness, patience, and so much more. And often, through the love of another human, we learn, just a small expression, of God's love for us.

This notion then brings us back to the point of being a whole person. If we're looking to a relationship to make us whole—to fill the hole, the gap, or the void—then maturity may always be a *mañana* thing, something we never achieve beyond a day. We never become that better helpmate, that person able to give effectively to someone else rather than being the one who needs everything done for us. All this leads to the fact that you can, perhaps even *should*, have romantic relationships (in a Christian context, of course) before you find the one you'll marry. The absence of consistent examples of healthy and lasting marriages has elevated dating to the arena where many develop relationship patterns.

In a Christian college, there's a lot of pressure, particularly in your junior and senior years to get or give a "ring by spring." After all, here's where you're supposed to meet that special someone. If not here, where? But there's also a lot of pressure placed on us by others. If you start hanging out with someone, maybe you actually go to a ballgame together or catch a flick you both want to see, suddenly the campus catches fire with news of your engagement. Right? We're back in junior high. "Guess who's going out with whom? I saw them walking hand in hand." If you just start showing a little exclusivity, not dates, just exclusivity; if you spend time together, friends and enemies stamp you as lovers in it for the long haul. You've all experienced that, I'm sure.

On the occasion of a "twerp" date, when the woman initiates and pays, the nuptials can't be more than a few weeks away. Frankly, I like it that these days the girls initiate and pay sometimes. It gives the guys a break, puts a little less pressure on the psyche and the wallet. As a guy, it's hard to always pick the right date venue. Not every girl likes hockey, the UFC, or a good action movie. Hard to believe but true. This gives the girls no excuse. They pick, they pay (so they know the budget constraints), and they find out of the guy is willing to enjoy. There are guys out there who like the theater or a chic flick, or at least are willing to pretend they do because they know you do. This gives the girl the opportunity to identify one of those guys. It's romantic too. The girl gets to pick the guy up, maybe bring him the rose, or choose an event he likes but has been a little afraid to invite the girl to. It tells him something very important. First, that he's special and second, the girl is willing to sacrifice a little—time, money, and emotion—to be with him.

Now that's not to say women become the guy or initiator in the relationship. No. You're still a vibrant attentive woman, and he's still a giving-caring man. He still opens the door for you, compliments your looks, and comes to your defense, if defense is necessary. But in those elements of the date that tell him he's special. As he's been using those same elements to tell you you're special, you pony up—buy the movie tickets, the popcorn, find a seat he's comfortable with.

But what about relationships that don't fit into this mold? The relationship where each pays for himself or herself, for instance. You go together to a movie but you meet at the theater, you buy your own ticket, buy your own popcorn, then you head to your own cars afterward. This goes on for months, even years. I've heard of it even going on into marriage. Each has a personal bank account, there's no sharing of assets or liabilities.

Or how about the relationship where the girl has to do everything, make all the plans, pay for everything (because she has the job), do all the driving, while the guy merely shows up. These relationships may be characteristic of a lack of maturity. Neither is willing to risk. Neither is willing to act like an adult. Guys will hang out with you, call and text you, follow you around like a puppy. But never ask you out. But if I ask you out, you may say no. Maturity says I'm secure enough in my relationship with the God and understand my own place in the world enough to risk disappointment, or even hurt. Immaturity demands you remain distant friends or even separate account mates. And instead of standing eye to eye and asking someone out for a date, you pass a piece of paper to his or her friend. "Do you think she'd go out with me?"

Maturity also tells you where you are in a relationship and manages expectations. As this young lady said in one of our classes: "Like I'm a freshman and my first boyfriend, like if he weren't making such a big deal about it, like it's not like you have to marry the first guy who comes along, like it's one date. Like, it's not a big deal. If you want to, like go with a lot of friends and the girls ask. It's not a big deal. The guys just make it a big deal."

This young lady alludes to the two parts to a sound relationship. One, the part of initiator and the other, who carries the responsibility. It matters which role you play. Experience has taught me that most men want to have the leadership role in their relationship but don't take it. Or fumble badly when they do. And for good reason, they may not know what that role looks like. Unfortunately, a lot of young men have never seen a man lead in an appropriate way. Their fathers were not spiritually mature men who could lead many times because their grandfathers weren't either.

Men without role models become too dominant, too chauvinistic, too threatened by a woman's strength and sense of purpose or too enabling to her weaknesses. He allows her to wear the pants because fighting her costs too much. His love is timid, weak, or insipid, rather than bold and masculine. If that's the model you've grown up with, why wouldn't you have a hard time defining your godly manhood and knowing how to lead?

Women, you need to allow the guy to be the leader. That's your part of maturity, of developing to where you have enough security in the Lord and your place in the universe so you can risk disappointment and hurt and take your place as help mate. He says, "I'm not sure if she wants me." And I say, "You'll never be sure about anybody."

Lasting and healthy relationships make us vulnerable to hurt and disappointments. We are only capable of taking risks in relationships when we are secure in our faith, depending upon and trust in God. He alone is always faithful and worthy of our complete surrender and dependence. When he heals and brings wholeness to our lives our life then becomes His story. A story of redemption that we can share openly, becoming transparent people, vulnerably allowing other to see what has been healed inside.

MINE, YOURS, AND OURS

The concept of mine, yours, and ours means in every relationship there are three parts. We can illustrate this in a couple different ways. Everyone brings a history to relationships—your family origins, personality, and past experiences. And when you're in a new relationship, you're going to bring some of your history to it. Your relationship history is what you bring that's good, or it can be past struggles and unhealthy patterns.

Maybe you grew up in a home that was verbally or physically abusive. I can illustrate this unfortunately from my own experience. My mother was very big into the corporal punishment thing. What I mean by that is not just a spanking but using something like a razor strop when we were growing up. As a result, a sibling decided they would never use any type of physical discipline on their children, ever. No physical form of discipline was ever used. In fact, raising the voice was considered abusive. Her husband grew up in a home that did what I consider an appropriate level of discipline. Things such as time outs when a child needs to learn boundaries and healthy rules or redirecting them by moving their hands out of the way, or even spank on occasion. Again, two completely different backgrounds and origin, and they clash when it comes to a marital and parental relationship.

If you've been hurt or maybe had somebody violate your trust in the past, you're a little bit weary when you enter a new relationship, aren't you? You should be a little more cautious, right? You may have developed an emotional shell shock. You're afraid that the present relationships may once again let you down or cause you pain or harm so there is a deep rooted fear of being wounded again.

It is very common to project forward what happened in the past. So it's important to understand where people come from, isn't it? Because really, who we are today is shaped strategically by our experiences in the past. So every relationship has a "mine" part and a "your" part, and then when you come together, there are some particular things that individuals face together. That's why we use this mine, yours, and ours when approaching relationships in the present and future. In healthy and lasting relationships, everybody has to take responsibility for their choices and experiences. We have the ability to identify our own baggage and history that we bring to it because it will affect present relationship to some degree or another.

Now when I talk about mine, yours, and ours, another whole category can be opened up that we don't cover with much detail in this book; that is the difference between men and women. I was having a conversation recently on the phone with somebody who is frustrated because of the tendencies of his wife to make decisions differently than he does. And I was trying to encourage him that the difference is not simply between he and his wife; the difference is between being a man and a woman. There's a theoretical 80/20 type rule. About 80 percent of women fit some certain characteristics and about 20 percent do not. About 80 percent of men fit certain characteristics and about 20 percent don't. It's not a universal truth, but there are general male/female characteristics that can be fairly characterized.

I think most people acknowledge that there are some unique differences between men and women. There's a popular book *Men Are from Mars, Women Are from Venus*, right? That's the whole concept. We live on two different planets. And so when it comes to mine, yours, and ours, we have to identify some of those things, because if we don't identify them as those legitimate differences that have to be addressed, the tendency is to personalize it. You're this way because you're married to me. Or I'm feeling this frustration because I'm married to you. And the reality of it is, it's just part of the experience of having a relationship. There's always a "mine," there's always a "yours," and there's always an "ours." Let me illustrate one more way.

I came from a home where communication was a one-way street. What I mean is, my father modeled for me in the marriages he had that if something was wrong, you should verbalize it. If something was wrong, it should be expressed. But if something was right, you didn't say anything. That's something I brought to the relationship with Roxanna. It didn't matter who I was going to marry. Whoever I married, I would have still started that way. Speak when something is wrong, be silent when everything is okay! Roxanna came from a home that had different style of communication that she brought to our relationship. It was easy for her to take that trait personally and believe that I, as a person, just can't articulate things that are positive or encouraging. When I married her, my communication style came with me. But I have to be able to address that honestly and take responsibility for how my style affects my wife. She has to take responsibility for how she receives my communication based on her learned style. She had to learn not to take things so personally. It wasn't personal. It was just a type, a style not directed at her. We both play a part in understanding our relationship history and building a health and lasting relationship together.

I had to get over some of my learned tendencies. I had to understand there are times you just need to form the words and speak something that's positive. Another aspect is that Roxanna had to develop the understanding of my tendencies. So when I'm silent, don't think something is automatically wrong. In fact, silence may mean everything's really good. It's an understanding of knowing where I'm coming from, and I know where she's coming from.

To illustrate that a little further, I remember my stepmom would try to get my dad to give her positive verbal affirmations.

He was always good about communicating when something was wrong, but when something was right, he wouldn't say it. One of the things she would do is she that she would solicit a positive response. Soliciting in a relationship means trying to get a person to do something, manipulating a conversation to get a desired outcome. She would say things, such as "Do you like the stroganoff tonight, Glen?" And he'd say, "Um, it's okay." And that wasn't enough because it wasn't the type of affirmation and acknowledgement she wanted. She wanted him to say, "I've been eating beef stroganoff of yours and from other people for many years, but this beef stroganoff is the best beef stroganoff that any human being in history has ever prepared! And furthermore, I am blessed of all men to be married to a woman that would be able to create such a cuisine that would be for kings and princes!" She wanted acknowledged and needed verbal affirmation.

My dad died a few years ago, but when I go to visit my step-mom, it's still the same thing. She's still trying to solicit people's affirmation, and it doesn't matter who she's talking to or who comes to visit. It doesn't matter what relationship she's in. She needs that because affirmation is a human need. It is a human characteristic to desire to be approved and appreciated.

I want to encourage you to seek premarital counseling if you're thinking about marrying somebody. It's important for you to identify what the tendencies or family of origin matters you're bringing to the relationship so they can be identified at the outset. Not that those things are going to change the decision to marry initially, but so they can be addressed. In parts of our society, it's often made a joking matter that men are strong but often way too silent when it comes to positive communication. It is an important thing to identify and take responsibility because men can do something about it. They can intentionally develop habits of communicating positively to those around them rather than just live with being the "silent type." This awareness and responsibility can begin in a healthy premarital counseling environment.

Let's consider other examples of things people bring to relationships that are important to grasping the concept of mine, yours, and ours.

At times, people who are not very secure in their personal identity or God-given value will minimize everything. Someone could say, "You really look nice," and they respond with, "I know but my hair is not right." Or when you say, "You look very nice in that dress," the reply might be "it's not the dress I really wanted to wear or the outfit I really wanted to wear." They minimize everything stated positive to degrade themselves, rejecting positive statement and reinforcements. In a long lasting relationship, this tendency can be very challenging. Sometimes, a person may stop giving much needed affirmations when they are minimized or rejected.

There are certain cultures that impact relationships. I was counseling a couple awhile back, and the husband claimed he came from a long lineage of what he called "proud Italian arguers." At the family table, they would argue and argue and argue. Given his family culture, which I don't know that it's necessarily an Italian tendency, but he perceived it that way. But in his perception, that was a proud Italian characteristic. He went on to explain that by the time the meal is over, no one is upset about anything. His family could argue and things could escalate emotionally very quickly. They could go back and forth and all use loud and angry voices, but he says it doesn't affect their relationship.

Well, if you don't come from that background and someone's talking in a loud tone of voice and making gestures that fly at your personal space, if that's not your culture, how does that feel to you? It's scary and it's not normal.

A student coming from a Hispanic culture told me there's a distinct impact of "machismo" in their family. Macho is the concept of clearly delineated man's role in the family. Other cultures don't have the same perception so culture does affect roles of men and women. These differences are seen in the roles of husbands and wives when it comes to parenting. There are things in some cultures that men do and don't do and others that they are more intimately involved in parenting and child rearing.

If you have in-laws where the mother-in-law is the matriarch and you don't come from that background, it may be a real point of contention. There's not only people group cultures; there are obviously individual family culture. You have family culture characteristics in your family. It's important to identify them as those things are going to come out down the road. Differences among people don't necessarily endear us to each other. You might have heard the expression, "Opposites attract"? I would say that there's maybe some curiosity and some attraction to opposites in long-term relationships but seven small sharp differences can present real challenges. It is the pebble in the shoe concept; even the smallest items can become painful over time.

These are reasons why it's strategic to understand the different roles we play. The different aspects of our relationship to one another—the mine, yours, and ours. What are some of the characteristics of your family that you can identify, the things *you* bring to your relationships? Consider family traditions when it comes to holidays. You say these things really don't impact relationships. You bet they do. When it comes to your family culture, what do you do for Thanksgiving?

I was visiting with my stepmother just over the Thanksgiving break, and my dad's family were all in from Ohio. When it comes to dressing, they don't have dressing up north; they have something called stuffing. Stuffing is taking bread and "stuffing" it inside the turkey and baking it. It's literally inside the turkey when it's cooked with the gizzard and other intestinal parts! Dressing is something people put in a pan and they bake it in an oven. Dressing consists of cornbread, sage, and other seasonings moist on the inside and crispy on the outside. I was only married for a few years and my dad's mother came down from the north to visit for Thanksgiving. An important relationship issue came up when the question was posed—"Who's going to make the stuffing/dressing?" Lucille, my dad's mom, had some pretty strong opinions about what dressing is supposed to be like, and it did impact my parent's relationship for thirty years.

In your home, when do you celebrate Christmas? Is it a Christmas Eve family gathering? Or is it a Christmas all day event? Many people think Christmas should be celebrated on Christmas morning only. Some people actually come from a strange background. They open all their presents on Christmas Eve. Some may open up one present on Christmas Eve, but it can't be certain presents. It's usually one of those secondary or trivial gifts from Uncle Bill or Aunt Lucy. You know, the ones that aren't too strategic. In a perfect world, you bake the cookies and we listen to Chipmunks throughout the entire week, that's my tradition. My spouse comes from a little bit different tradition. Who is right and who is wrong when it comes to family traditions? Lasting and healthy relationships recognize traditions matter to all of us.

How do you do birthdays? I met a couple awhile back where he came from a home that on their birthday, his privilege was to stay in bed all day where everyone tended to him and and serve. That was his birthday tradition and expectation. Please understand I don't think it's a bad concept necessarily, but if you don't come from that background, it may present relationship challenges. Your birthday practice may be that everyone comes over for a big meal where it's about people instead of you being in bed and everybody brings dinner to you. That takes getting used to, doesn't it? And then you wrap them all together in a relationship! I'm talking about holidays, birthdays, and anniversaries, and what you do on Memorial Day weekend and Labor Day weekend! You can see how those differences are not necessarily going to endear you to others. You've got to work through them with understanding and a willingness to make changes and sacrifice, at times, your personal preferences.

Here's the bottom line about mine, yours, and ours. It doesn't matter who you marry. It doesn't matter who you date. There's going to be differences. So the question is do you recognize the real sources of relationship tensions and challenges?

Differences pose challenges when it comes to house rules. It may either be spoken rules or unspoken rules you grew up with. Every family has this unspoken list of rules, and they aren't written down either. And you don't realize the rule is even there until you break it! For example, in Roxanna's family, the rule was you don't ever talk about money. She made the mistake one time of asking her grandma how much her purse was, and she was immediately shushed and shamed. Unspoken rule: Don't ever ask anybody how much something cost. She married a guy where in his home, it was a frequent subject at the dinner table. Family gatherings are quite interesting.

In Roxanna's home many conversations had sexual contexts to them because she grew up on a farm. The cows were reproducing each year, even the pigs and the chickens were doing it! Sex was just everywhere on the farm. It wasn't this sacred or private thing; it was just a part of life. It was just how they lived. It was just down to earth and nitty-gritty and then when it came time for the farmer to tell the farmer's daughter about sex, it too lacked tenderness. She married into my family where we didn't talk about sex at all. When I went to the family farm, the jokes were flying about what and how the bulls were doing it and how often. I thought they were just sex-crazed people!

Think about the rules in the home you grew up with. Either they were spoken rules such as don't ever talk about money or it was so embedded and imprinted on you that sex was everywhere so everybody was talking about it, and that's considered status quo healthy. Those types of rules are going to be integrated into relationship for the rest of your life and may be passed on to your children.

I want to mention one more aspect. Values are formed through mine, yours, and ours as well. We all have them engrained in us from our families and life experiences. It doesn't matter if you had one or two parents in the home or if you were raised by your grandparents. We were all given certain values. Some may be like the value of not talking about money. But when it comes to finances, that value will impact all relationships when you're dating and/or when you're married.

I grew up in a home where my dad was an iron worker. We were a family that worked manual/industrial labor. We had less resources than some so we viewed possessions and resources from that reference point. If you don't have a lot of discretionary money to spend, you tend to carefully scrutinize how and when money is spent. An example of a money rule I grew up with is that when something is on sale, you buy it. If it is a really good sale, you buy as many as you can, whether you needed them or not! You bought a lot because it was cheap.

Roxanna grew up in a different home. Her parents owned a business. They were not wealthy people, but they did not have to think so often or so critically about whether or not to spend money. When we were newly married, it didn't take long for our different values concerning money to surface. She sent me to the grocery store to buy two cans of Del Monte green beans. When I get to the store and start looking at Del Monte green beans, I noticed they're two cans for a dollar. Then I look over and I see this yellow label brand! They are four cans for a dollar! Why would I spend all that crazy money on two cans of green beans when I can get four of them for a buck? Value.

I don't know that my dad ever said, "Okay, here's how shopping for green beans should be done." But it's true that parents and family members make comments that reinforce their values. My dad would see somebody in a new car and say, "You know, people spend a lot of money on a new car! But you know, these olds cars will get you around just as good as a good used one. They're just wasting their money on a new car." Values.

I heard my parents say, "Rich people just waste money on stuff like fancy name brand clothing at Macy's or Nordstrom. They just have more money than they have common sense." I remember confronting this value regarding money a few years ago. A value my dad gave me was you never spend more than $30 on a pair of shoes. No man in his right mind would buy a pair of shoes for more than thirty bucks. At that time, I worked as an administrator at a university where I wore dress shoes every day. I would wear out one pair of $25 shoes every year and my feet were chronically painful. Roxanna and I were shopping one day and we saw a pair of men's dress shoes on sale for $80. My immediate response to her suggestion to buy them was absolutely not! Sale? Yes! $80.

As the conversation progressed Roxanna said, "Why don't you just try them and see how they last?"

I'll never forget purchasing that pair of $80 shoes and wearing and wearing and wearing them. And they didn't hurt my feet! I thought I'd never wear those shoes out. It dawned on me that there might be something to the crazy notion that Roxanna asserted. "Sometimes, you get what you pay for." There are many values concerning money and at least two truths. You don't always get what you pay for, that's one truth. Another truth is, sometimes you do get what you pay for.

To make this values difference even more complex, we have to consider that in some homes, love and affections were given though gifts and purchases and for good behavior. That will kill a relationship before it ever gets started as you can't attach love to performance or gifts or values.

Our values are not necessarily right or wrong, or something to judge. However, lasting and healthy relationships learn to recognize the mine, yours, and ours differences.

OUR WORDS AND RELATIONSHIPS

We must deal with the power of our words and how they affect relationships. I'm not speaking of mere communication as a style or method. In order to create and maintain healthy and lasting relationships, we must manage the tone and emotional power of our words. The term *manage* reflects the scriptural concept that the book of James in the New Testament discusses regarding the tongue. "No man can tame the tongue, it is a world of fire." The images giving Scripture regarding the tongue and our control over the words we use are vivid and accurate. One comparison is to a bridle or bit which is put into a horse's mouth to control the beast. Another compares the tongue to a rudder, which determines the direction of large vessels upon the ocean fighting the currents and waves. The emphasis of these metaphors is upon the reality that human beings struggle with control of the tongue. While no one can tame the tongue completely, we can gain a measure of control over our words.

In close relationships, like parent-child, husband-wife, or close friends and associates, our words are enduring. A child who is told repeatedly they are worthless and stupid will develop into an adult who believes it. Developmentally, a child or adolescent hearing a well-timed or frequent "You will never amount to anything" may become a self-fulfilling prophecy. In marriages where a spouse frequently points out mistakes or inadequacies, a real sense of never being enough can be debilitating. When the hope of pleasing or achieving is gone, the motivation vanishes as well.

The mood and tone of relationships are influenced by the words we speak to one another. A loose tongue can determine the course of a relationship. People will use expressions such as "I spoke out of turn," "I shot my mouth off," "I verbally vomited," or "I was just blowing off steam." But to the recipient of these verbal barrages, the emotional effects are wounding and the damage is often permanent. Whether it is an emotional outburst or a constant pounding of verbal criticisms, relationships are built up or torn down by our words.

Learning to say what's true, kind, and necessary can serve to filter out what is helpful and beneficial, both in positive circumstances as well as negative ones. We are challenged in the Scriptures to speak the truth in love to one another. Truthfulness deals in part with not misrepresenting or lying but it also means that we are careful not to exaggerate. The frequent usage of *always* and *never* when communicating signifies frustration and often leads to exasperation.

In counseling dialogues, spouses will make statement such as "Kim *never* follows through on anything!" or "Bob *always* defends his family's sick behaviors." At times, I can visibly see the emotional exasperation. Parents are in a particular powerful position when they choose their words. When a child hears, "Why don't you ever, ever do what I ask you to do!" Their spirit is deflated, quenched, and at times, crushed. The words we use, along with our tone, facial expressions, and intensity, are emotionally powerful to build up or tear others down. In lasting and healthy relationships, there is a conscious and ongoing effort to tame tongues.

In addition to truthfulness, healthy and lasting relationships are characterized by kindness in speech. Paul describes in his letter to the church at Corinth that one of the key attributes of love is kindness. There are many things that we need to communicate to those closest to us; the things that we say may indeed be the truth. Truth spoken in love with kindness has the greatest opportunity to be heard and received.

I've known individuals that speak what is on their mind and wear that trait as a badge of honor! When confronted about their brash comments or expressive criticism they defend their position by simply saying, "Well, it's the truth." In relationships, it should be noted that perception becomes what we believe to be true or real. Healthy relationships must develop the ability to express concerns, frustrations, and even criticism in a kind manner. Kindness in speech refers to the words we use, the tone and volume of our voice, along with our body language. There are indeed times when we need to have difficult conversations with those closest to us, but even the most difficult conversations can be seasoned with kindness.

A third area to be considered when managing our tongues in relationships is saying things that are not necessary. As mentioned, healthy relationships do speak the truth to one another tempered by kindness or love. Making unnecessary commentary or corrections to those nearest to us will only create emotional distance. Unnecessary commentary would be correcting someone when they speak in error. An example would be verbally correcting your spouse or child when they erroneously identify an upcoming event. Does it really matter if the second Saturday in May is the 28 rather than the 27? We often make mistakes when it comes to dates, directions, or even names of past acquaintances. But pointing out when someone speaks in error or out of turn is not an endearing relationship characteristic.

There are times that it is caring and kind to point out errors. For example, when a date is pending a strategic engagement or family event where planning and schedules are involved. If it's a matter were of health or well-being of someone is concerned, reminding someone of their mistakes over matters of insignificance serves no relationship value.

The most frequent forms of unnecessary conversation come in the form of sarcasm when sarcastic remarks or jokes are made about an individual or their behaviors. While sarcasm may at

times seem like an innocent type of fun humor, it is rarely spoken without the cost being paid by someone emotionally.

One of the modern translations of Paul's letter to the church at Corinth describing love says, "True love hardly ever notices when others do things wrong." Verbally reminding someone of trivial mistakes or errors is not speaking the truth in love.

We discussed three ways we can create and maintain healthy relationships by managing our tongues. Speaking truthfully to another, kindness in tone, volume and body language, and only saying things that are necessary. It has been noted that the Scripture teaches us that no one is perfect in what they say. Therefore, our conversations in healthy and lasting relationships must include expressions of seeking forgiveness for our words. When we do speak exaggerations or generalizations and see the exasperation or realize we have hurt another, it is imperative that we take responsibility for our words.

When it comes to reconciling relationships from harm caused by our words, less is more. A simple and straightforward "I am sorry for generalizing by saying you never remember to call before you arrive home late, please forgive me for not speaking truth-truthfully or "I was wrong to say you were stupid, please forgive me for saying such an unkind thing to you."

Relationships that have created and maintained emotional intimacy are characterized by frequent expressions of sorrow for words ill-spoken.

Let's turn our attention now to the positive ways words can build and strengthen lasting relationships. While you are managing, our tongue primarily has to do with avoiding saying things that would hurt or tear down people. It is also a matter of intentional discipline to speak words that build and encourage. Every human being desires to be around people who verbally encourage and uplift. Every spouse needs to hear of their mates love on a consistent basis. Every child needs to know their parents love through verbal expression as well as actions.

I grew up in a home were verbal expressions of love were absent. There were times when my mother would solicit from my father and expression of love. My dad's family and many in his generation were not free to express and say the words *I love you.* When asked directly about his love, his default response was, "You know that I love you because I get up and go to work every day in order to care for you." While working hard and providing for our families is an expression of love, hearing the words matter.

I was in my mid-twenties the first time I heard my dad say out loud the words *I love you, son.* Prior to that time, all that I ever heard was his reply, "I love you too." That fall day many years ago opened my heart to my father, a heart that had been closed and hardened by many years without verbal affection. Thankfully, from that point forward until the day he passed from this earth, unsolicited expressions of love became more frequent. In healthy and lasting relationships, love is a matter of show and tell.

There is tremendous relationship power in verbal affirmations. In my experiences, few people pass through their lives surrounded by people who offer consistent verbal encouragement. I have one dear lifelong friend that I consider to have the gift of encouragement. Dan is one of those individuals that people are drawn to relationally. His family, work associates, and even casual acquaintances are all beneficiaries of this kind and endearing spoken affirmations. He seems to always have something positive worth saying about the people he is with. Dan has been an effective role model for me showing how to manage my speech and deliver life-giving words.

As discussed in a previous chapter, I grew up in a home where silence was the rule. If something was wrong, everyone was quick to articulate. If something was right or even great there was only silence. While we all have our families of origins and natural tendencies, we can develop habits of verbal affirmation. We could start by taking advantage of Hallmark! It may be difficult for us to formulate the words of kindness and affirmation but a trip to the pharmacy or grocery store and a few minutes of reading can provide fodder and ideas for our expressions of value and worth to others. We could begin by actually buying those cards that express gratitude, affection, and positive affirmations and deliver them to those closest to us.

A quick search of the Internet will reveal specific sites with words of poetry, affirmation, and encouragement. You could send text messages, leave a sticky note, write on the mirror in your home with lipstick, or leave a voicemail message with words that give life. The Scriptures full of spiritual affirmations and prayers that can be delivered to those nearest and dearest.

If you desire to develop healthy and lasting relationships, make it your goal to consistently (daily) speak or send life-giving affirmations to those around you. Your spouse, boyfriend, girlfriend, roommate, or work associates will appreciate you and become endeared. Begin by making a list of those closest to you. Develop reminders in your smartphone to remind you. Utilize words and expressions of others until you become more fluent as an encourager in writing and in your own spoken words.

Another way in which our words can impact our relationships is to provide healing. In close and intimate relationships, such as marriage and parenting, words have the power to assist in the healing.

A few years ago my wife and I attended a conference for pastors and their spouses hosted by Dr. David and Teresa Ferguson. Their organization Intimate Life Ministries hosted a weekend retreat at a conference center in Northern California. A significant part of the weekend was focusing upon the concept of *helpmates that heal*. Dr. Ferguson developed the concept that one aspect of being a lifemate is to be a helpmate that heals. We were given the assignment of going out on a walk together and articulating to each other a painful memory from our past.

I recall describing to Roxanna a painful physical and emotional experience. I was about ten years old, playing as boys do in my father's garage. I had been warned on many occasions never to attempt opening closing my father's coveted and very large upright toolbox. On this particular day, I was trying to assemble a motorcycle that I had purchased, and most of the engine parts were in a box. I was in need of a three-sixteenths-inch box-end wrench. My father had left for a few moments to get some parts for the dump truck that he was working on that day. Impatient as ten-year-old boys are, instead of waiting for my father to return, I decided to attempt to lift the large metal-hinged cover to retrieve the wrench. As warned the task was too much for my small body to handle, it dropped closed on my hand slicing open my second finger of my right hand.

When my father returned home, I was huddled on the ground floor holding my finger tightly to slow down the bleeding. As was the case in my family when someone was injured, there was blame to be placed upon someone. I was verbally scolded before being spanked for not obeying his instructions prior to being taken to the hospital for stitches. The painful part for me that I expressed to Roxanna that day was that I simply needed to be comforted. I had disobeyed and was experiencing the consequences, but when children are hurt, they need comfort. Could be in the form of words that assure or a simple hug and gentle caress. I had received neither.

I had been carrying that memory with me for nearly thirty years. That experience had affected me as a boy, as a man, and as a father. I gasped for air while sobbing. Roxanna placed her hand on my face and brushed away the tears. She said out loud to me, "I'm so sorry, that pain you felt then and feel now. Know that if I were there, I would've hugged and comforted you as I am doing so now." I felt in my spirit a sense of calm and comfort upon hearing her statements. I experienced a profound measure of healing that day.

Our words have a power to give comfort and bring healing to life's deepest hurts. The closer the relationship, the more power. Parents can speak words of healing to their children. Spouses can become helpmates that heal. You can be the friend that administers the verbal healing balm. You can be the neighbor or work associate that speaks grace and comfort in a time of need.

When someone close to you has received a catastrophic notification regarding an accident, sudden death, or a dismal prognosis, our tendency may be to speak to encourage saying things such as "I know what you're going through" or "don't worry, all things work together for those who love the Lord." These well intended but trite explanations offer no comfort at all. In times of crisis, people don't want or need theological explanations or identification with their experience. What matters is hearing the words, "I'm so sorry," while receiving that gentle touch or hug. After we have administered verbal consolation, the day might come to give instruction or perspective. Words have the power in relationships to promote healing and to give comfort.

The words we choose when expressing our feelings and emotions will determine how well we will be heard. The expression "Say what you mean and mean what you say" is a valuable axiom for relationships. Healthy and lasting relationships develop clear conversational practices. Clear communication articulates directly without coding. Unhealthy relationships rely upon codes to reflect what they mean rather than saying that which needs to be communicated.

I have an aunt who is a master of communication coding. My uncle would ask her, "Do you have any problems with me playing golf next Saturday?" Her standard reply would be, "Well, that's just fine with me." The words she used gave permission for the golf outing, but the tone of her voice and the rolling of her eyes indicated her disapproval. Over time, individuals can become adept at deciphering conversational codes, but healthy and lasting relationships practice clear and direct communication.

Other examples of communication coding would be the use of the expressions such as "So that's how it's going to be," "You can do whatever you want," or, one of my favorites, "How's that working for you?" Saying what you mean and meaning what you say facilitates clear communication avoiding misunderstandings, leaving no room for coded messages.

There are times in all relationships when we must communicate things that really bug us. We are now going to look at ways to express things that are really irritating us to others. Healthy and lasting relationships do not carry around penned up frustrations or irritations. There is an effective way to communicate things that really bug us with the people whom we love. As discussed early on in this chapter, there are times we must simply overlook or accept idiosyncrasies. However, if certain behaviors or habits become an ongoing source of relationship irritation, they must be articulated. It's the pebble of the shoe concept; it may seem like a very small item and insignificant to be expressed, but the longer you go down the relationship road, the small issue becomes much larger in its impact.

When it's time to discuss the things that are bothering you with those whom you love, you must choose the setting carefully. Timing is important. Be certain that you do not bring up difficult subjects on the way out of the door to work or right before falling off to sleep. In general, when people are well rested and not under scheduling pressures, they are more receptive.

The place you choose to have these conversations matters as well. Never bring up the things that bother you in the presence of others. Make these conversations private and with consideration to whether there might be interruptions.

Another item to consider would be the emotional climate of the person to whom you will be expressing the things that are bothering you. Emotional climate is outside factors that would hinder effective communication. The acronym HAT serves as a measure or thermostat to consider when not to bring up the issues. When a person is *hungry*, they tend to be more irritable and impatient and not in a position to hear your concerns. If someone is *angry* after the drive home in traffic or receiving some bad news, it is not a good opportunity to process frustrations. When people are *tired* and fatigued, their emotional thresholds are taxed, and the ability to listen and hear without defensiveness is compromised.

Now that we've considered the circumstances and the setting for effective relationship communication, let's consider how we say what's really bugging us. The same principle presented when offering an apology or reconciling malicious speech applies. Less is more. The most effective relationship communication is simple, short, and specific. For instance, "Tom, I am really bugged when you leave your dirty clothes on the floor. I feel like you believe it is my job to pick up after you." Stop. Remember more is less, and as we discussed earlier, do not generalize by using the terms always or never. When Tom hears "Why do you always leave your dirty clothes around? or "You never help around the house by picking up your dirty clothes." The communication is received as you always do it wrong and you never do it right.

When articulating the things that are bothersome to you in relationships, there is no need to illustrate. We may be tempted to cite all the recent transgressions, but our concerns are heard more effectively when they stand alone.

Practicing effective relationship communication skills will create and maintain healthy and lasting associations. It is important to note that in the closest earthly relationships we must endeavor to love imperfections. We cannot change others; we only have the capacity with God's power to see change brought to our own lives.

The final item that we will consider in our discussion of how our words affect relationships and that our words have the power to bestow treasures. I have a large nondescript box next to my bed; it is my treasure box. If I ever have to flee in the case of a fire in my home, the one item that I would grab to carry out safely would be that box. My treasure box contains no items of gold, silver, or any precious stones. It holds only paper. Some are pictures drawn by little hands expressed by tender young hearts. Most of the treasures are cards, sticky notes, or handwritten letters scribbled on miscellaneous size and shaped papers.

All of my treasures were given to me by those I love—my wife, my daughter Gabrielle, my son Greyson, and brothers and sisters in Christ. The specific content written to me has rarely been shared with anyone. When I receive a new treasure, I read it, take it into my heart, and then place it in my box. There are times I go back to my box when I'm feeling alone or hurting in some way. I will reread or look at the pictures and there find the treasure of expressed love that soothes and comforts.

Many of my most valued treasures were created by the hands of my loved ones. My wife passed on to my daughter and interest along with an amazing creative spirit to produce handmade cards. My son has taken ordinary household items and transformed them into love letters and messages of appreciation. Each is original works of art and personalized for the occasion—birthdays, Christmas, Father's Day, anniversaries of happy and sad events, special achievements, Valentine's Day, or Happy Day Cards given out only on days of the week, which end in the letter Y.

The spoken word has the power to build up, encourage, and heal, but the written word can be an enduring treasure. Giving these treasures does not require financial or a great amount of time resources. You can begin by relying on the creativity of others by a visit to a retail store that stocks cards for all occasions. You can purchase stationary that you can decorate to personalize along with your words of expressed value and love. With a little time and intentional effort, you can bestow treasures upon those you love.

I cannot express strongly enough the value of written treasures. If you have ever been the recipient of these types of treasures, you know their value. I've instructed my wife to bury the content of my treasure box with me. I believe that that written treasures are eternal gifts, and as our bodies will perish along with paper and wooden boxes, our earthly relationships are deepened eternally when we give and receive written treasures of love, appreciation, and value. In relationships, our words matter.